Atonement

by Ian McEwan

David James

Series Editors:
Nicola Onyett and Luke McBratney

HODDER
EDUCATION
AN HACHETTE UK COMPANY

The publisher would like to thank the following for permission to reproduce copyright material:

Acknowledgments:

Ian McEwan: from *Atonement*, published by Jonathan Cape. Reproduced by permission of The Random House Group Ltd.**; pp.19,41,52,54,58,59: Daniel Zalewski:** from 'The Background Hum' from *The New Yorker* (The New Yorker, 23rd February 2009), Daniel Zalewski/The New Yorker; © Condé Nast; **p.26: Geoff Dyer:** from 'Who's afraid of influence?' from *The Guardian* (The Guardian, 22nd September 2001), copyright Guardian News & Media Ltd 2001; **p.33: Ian McEwan:** from 'Ian McEwan' (British Humanist Association, 2015); **pp.31,33: Helen Whitney:** from 'Faith and Doubt at Ground Zero. Interviews - Ian McEwan' from *PBS* (Frontline, April 2002); **p.35: Ian McEwan** adapted from 'Ian McEwan: the law versus religious belief' from *The Guardian* (The Guardian, 5th September 2014); **pp.38,57,60–1,62: Jonathan Noakes and Margaret Reynolds:** taken from an interview, featured in *Ian McEwan: The Essential Guide* (Vintage, 2011); **p.56: Zadie Smith:** from 'Zadie Smith [English Novelist, Born 1975] Talks With Ian McEwan [English Novelist, Born 1948] from *The Believer* (The Believer, August 2005); **p.57: Charles McGrath:** from 'ON WRITERS AND WRITING; Not Quite Right for Our Pages' from *The New York Times* (The New York Times, 27th October 2002) ; **p.64: David Sexton:** from 'McEwan's Finest Shock Tactics Yet' from *The Evening Standard* (The Evening Standard, September 2001); **p.64: Michiko Kakutani:** from 'BOOKS OF THE TIMES; And When She Was Bad She Was …' from *The New York Times* (The New York Times, 7th March 2002); **p.64: Frank Kermode:** from 'Point of View' from *London Review of Books, Vol. 23 No. 19* (London Review of Books, 4th October 2001); **p.64: Hermione Lee:** from 'If your memories serve you well…', from *The Guardian* (The Guardian, 23rd September 2001), copyright Guardian News & Media Ltd 2001.

Every effort has been made to trace or contact all copyright holders, but if any have been inadvertently overlooked the Publishers will be pleased to make the necessary arrangements at the first opportunity.

Photo credits:

p.vi Artwork © Chris Frazer Smith. Used by arrangement with The Random House Group Limited; **p.2** © FOCUS FEATURES / THE KOBAL COLLECTION / BAILEY, ALEX; **p.5** © FOCUS FEATURES / THE KOBAL COLLECTION / BAILEY, ALEX; **p.21** © MPI/Getty Images; **p.24** © Planet News Archive/SSPL/Getty Images; **p.29** Bettmann/CORBIS; **p. 35** © 505587937 - iStock via Thinkstock/Getty Images; **p.42** © Snap Stills/REX; **p.43** Focus/Everett /REX; **p.47** © Moviestore/REX; **p.56** © REX; **p.60** © David Hartley/REX; **p.61** © ITV/REX

Although every effort has been made to ensure that website addresses are correct at time of going to press, Hodder Education cannot be held responsible for the content of any website mentioned. It is sometimes possible to find a relocated web page by typing in the address of the home page for a website in the URL window of your browser.

Orders: please contact Bookpoint Ltd, 130 Milton Park, Abingdon, Oxon OX14 4SB. Telephone: (44) 01235 827720. Fax: (44) 01235 400454. Lines are open 9.00–17.00, Monday to Saturday, with a 24-hour message answering service. Visit our website at www.hoddereducation.co.uk

© David James 2016

First published in 2016 by

Hodder Education
An Hachette UK Company,
Carmelite House, 50 Victoria Embankment
London EC4Y 0LS

Impression number	5	4	3	2	1
Year	2020	2019	2018	2017	2016

Cover photo (and throughout) © abzee/istockphoto.com

Illustrations by Philip Allen

Typeset in 11/13pt Univers LT Std 47 Light Condensed by Integra Software Services Pvt. Ltd., Pondicherry, India

Printed in Italy

A catalogue record for this title is available from the British Library

ISBN 9781471853807

Contents

Using this guide

Why read this guide?

The purposes of this A-level Literature Guide are to enable you to organise your thoughts and responses to the text, deepen your understanding of key features and aspects and help you to address the particular requirements of examination questions and non-exam assessment tasks in order to obtain the best possible grade. It will also prove useful to those of you writing an NEA piece on the text as it provides a number of summaries, lists, analyses and references to help with the content and construction of the assignment.

Note that teachers and examiners are seeking above all else evidence of an *informed personal response to the text*. A guide such as this can help you to understand the text, form your own opinions, and suggest areas to think about, but it cannot replace your own ideas and responses as an informed and autonomous reader.

How to make the most of this guide

You may find it useful to read sections of this guide when you need them, rather than reading it from start to finish. For example, you may find it helpful to read the 'Contexts' section before you start reading the text, or to read the 'Part/ chapter summaries and commentaries' section in conjunction with the text – whether to back up your first reading of it at school or college or to help you revise. The sections relating to the Assessment Objectives will be especially useful in the weeks leading up to the exam.

Key elements

This guide is designed to help you to raise your achievement in your examination or Non-exam Assessment response to *Atonement*. It is intended for you to use throughout your AS/A-level English Literature course. It will help you when you are studying the novel for the first time and also during your revision.

The following features have been used throughout this guide to help you focus your understanding of the novel:

Context

Context boxes give contextual information that relates directly to particular aspects of the text.

TASK

Tasks are short and focused. They allow you to engage directly with a particular aspect of the text.

CRITICAL VIEW

Critical view boxes highlight a particular critical viewpoint that is relevant to an aspect of the main text This allows you to develop the higher-level skills needed to come up with your own interpretation of a text.

Build critical skills

Broaden your thinking about the text by answering the questions in the **Build critical skills** boxes. These help you to consider your own opinions in order to develop your skills of criticism and analysis.

Taking it further ▶▶

Taking it further boxes suggest and provide further background or illuminating parallels to the text.

Top ten quotation ◁ Top ten quotation

A cross-reference to Top ten quotations (see pages 94–98 of this guide), where each quotation is accompanied by a commentary that shows why it is important.

An unconventional novel

Atonement can be considered an unconventional piece of fiction clothed as a conventional novel. As we read, it appears to be a conventional, realist novel, written in the third person, about a family living in Surrey before the outbreak of the Second World War. But by the time we have finished it, our views of the text have changed profoundly. We discover, among many other things, that the novel is 'written' by the central character – Briony Tallis – and that the crime that she commits in falsely accusing Robbie Turner of raping Lola Quincey acts as the motivation for her seeking, but never finding, atonement.

The novel's structure

The novel is divided into four distinct sections: Part One, by far the longest section, is set in England in 1935; Part Two shifts to northern France during the British retreat at Dunkirk in 1940; Part Three is also set in 1940, on the 'Home Front' in London; the fourth section is entitled 'London 1999' and brings us up to date with all the major characters. With the exception of Part Two (which focuses on Robbie Turner's final days as he tries to escape German forces), each of these sections has Briony at their centre: we trace her life from being a young girl possessed with a vivid imagination, to being a probationer nurse in London during the war; and then, finally, we see her at 77 years old, a successful novelist coming to terms with being diagnosed with a form of dementia. The final part is her attempt to explain her actions, to ensure 'everything is in the right box file' and that there is 'a tidy finish'.

However, this process proves to be profoundly unsettling for the reader. *Atonement* challenges our expectations of what a novel – and the narrative it constructs – should consist of. It also subverts an unspoken rule between author and reader that the world constructed within the pages of the book has its own internal logic, and that the process of creating that is kept hidden by the writer from the reader. In Part Three Briony receives a letter from Cyril Connolly, which in itself is an intrusion from the 'real' world as Connolly was a respected and influential literary editor of the time. In this letter he criticises Briony's short story (*Two Figures by a Fountain*) which she has sent for publication in *Horizon* magazine. We then realise that he is referring to Part One of *Atonement*. It is the literary equivalent of a playwright, or actor, breaking down 'the fourth wall' between the stage and the audience. Nothing is the same again.

▲ What does the cover of this edition of *Atonement* convey to you?

It is from this point that the novel changes from the traditional narrative of Parts One and Two, to something postmodern: it is no longer only a story about the Tallis family, and Robbie's fate; instead it has become a novel about writing itself, an elaborate and sophisticated construction in which the main narrator is drafting and redrafting what we have read. Furthermore, she is doing so in order to revise the 'crime' that she, as a young girl, committed against Robbie Turner. This process of subversion continues to the very last page of the novel, scenes that moved us, such as Robbie and Cecilia's reunion in London, are revealed to be rewritings by Briony to gain atonement for herself, and to avoid 'the bleakest realism' of what actually happened. In achieving this state Briony hopes to gain not only forgiveness, but also something close to 'at-one-ment'. Exactly what McEwan's intentions were in constructing a novel like this remains deliberately ambiguous. Indeed the popularity of *Atonement* can partly be explained by this ambiguity, as well as the scale of its conceptual and literary ambition.

A critical and commercial success

Its popularity is no doubt largely down to this 'something', to the scale of its conceptual and literary ambition. But we should not make the mistake of concluding that it is *only* because of the originality of its structure, and the brilliance of its execution, that *Atonement* continues to be read, studied and enjoyed by so many readers. It contains some of McEwan's finest writing (Martin Amis believes that the first 200 pages of the novel are McEwan's greatest achievement). The depiction of a sweltering, rural England between the wars is startlingly vivid, threatening, sensuous and sensual, and Part Two is a protracted, visceral description of war, unflinching in its portrayal of violence. Our strongest emotions – including love, hate, compassion and forgiveness – are also explored with real power and sensitivity, and as McEwan is one of the most intellectual authors writing today, we are also challenged by complex ideas about consciousness, death, science and justice.

Beyond all this it is the characters themselves that make us read on: Briony, Robbie, Cecilia, Lola – each live on the page, and it is perhaps a lasting testimony to McEwan's skill as a writer that not only do they survive Briony's revelations at the end of the novel, but are actually enhanced by it. We are allowed to see Robbie and Cecilia reconciled, just for a few pages, before we learn of their cruel, lonely deaths. The author alone can grant us that privilege; that richness of emotions is not something we would sacrifice to 'what really happened'. We see them for all their faults, and from many different perspectives, and we learn about the times they lived and loved (and died) in. We also learn about *how* they were created. Whether we, as readers, can forgive McEwan for forcing us to reassess our relationships with his characters so radically remains a matter for each individual reader. But one thing is certain: *Atonement* is that rare thing, a book that demands to be reread because it can only be properly understood in doing so; it is also a book that is unlikely ever to be forgotten, whether you read it for pleasure, or as part of your A-level studies. It is a modern classic.

Part One begins on a hot summer's day in 1935: the Tallis family are waiting for their three cousins to arrive at their home in Surrey. The cousins – Lola (15), and twins Pierrot and Jackson (9) – are staying at the house while their parents (Hermione and Cecil) go through a difficult divorce. Emily Tallis (Hermione's elder sister) is unwell and has retired to her room. She is married to Jack who, because of his work as a senior civil servant in London, cannot attend the gathering. Emily's eldest daughter Cecilia is back from Cambridge after studying English Literature; her days are spent reading, and trying to find a career. The younger sister, Briony Tallis (13), has written a melodrama entitled *The Trials of Arabella* which she wants her cousins to perform. Leon, the oldest of the three Tallis children, is returning for the weekend with his friend, Paul Marshall, who is a successful chocolate-bar manufacturer. Also at the house is Robbie Turner. Like Cecilia he has just finished studying his degree in English at Cambridge, but unlike Cecilia (who gained a Third Class degree) he has graduated with a First. He has decided to go on to study medicine. Robbie is the son of the Tallis cleaner, Grace; and his studies have been paid for by Jack Tallis. Other characters present are servants, including the cook Betty, Hardman and his son Danny.

Rehearsals for the play do not go well, and are eventually abandoned by Briony. Meanwhile Cecilia has decided to put some wildflowers into a precious vase which she takes outside to the fountain for water; while there she gets into an argument with Robbie that results in the vase breaking. She strips down to her underwear in front of Robbie and retrieves the broken pieces from the water. Briony watches all of this from a window.

Lola, Pierrot and Jackson retreat to the playroom where they are eventually joined by Marshall, who flirts with Lola. Briony has stormed out of the house, plotting revenge on her cousins for ruining the play. Robbie has returned home and, although confused by Cecilia's behaviour at the fountain, recalls her beauty in adoring detail. He decides to write her a letter of apology, but in a moment of puerile humour, writes another, obscene letter, stating how much he would like to have sex with her. Distracted by the forthcoming dinner at the Tallis home, as well as thoughts about his future, he mistakenly takes *this* letter and, encountering Briony on the way, asks her to deliver it to Cecilia. He realises his terrible mistake, but it is too late: Briony has already raced ahead of him to the house and delivered the explicit letter.

Cecilia is interrupted by Lola who tells her that the twins have physically attacked her, and she shows the marks on her arms to prove it. Cecilia also realises how much the twins have been neglected since they arrived. Briony delivers the letter to her sister, and it is clear she has opened the letter and read it. Cecilia's response is not what Robbie had feared, and she draws him into the library where they begin to make love. They are interrupted by Briony who thinks that Robbie is attacking her sister. The family dinner is filled with tension and reaches a climax when a letter is discovered from the twins saying they have run away. A search ensues and Robbie decides to look for them alone. During the search Briony encounters a distraught Lola, and sees a departing figure whom she thinks is Robbie. Lola has been attacked, and probably raped. The police are called, and Briony shows them Robbie's letter to Cecilia. When Robbie returns (with the twins) he is arrested and charged with rape; Briony's witness statement is key to securing his conviction and jail sentence.

▲ The writing and reading of letters is a motif which runs through *Atonement*

Part Two begins in Dunkirk where, five years later, Robbie is leading two other men (Corporals Mace and Nettle) to the planned evacuation of British forces. Robbie has served three-and-a-half years of his sentence but has negotiated an early release to serve in the army. He has been injured by shrapnel and is becoming weaker, the longer he has to walk. The men rest overnight and are fed by two French farmers who tell him about the extent of the allied retreat. The next day the soldiers reach Dunkirk, but they do so after watching many people being injured and dying from attacks by the German Luftwaffe. As Robbie's injury worsens he thinks back to his time in England, and in particular his lasting love of Cecilia. He recalls how they met after he was released from jail: she is now a nurse and has broken off all relations with her family because of their treatment of him. She writes to him that Briony has turned down a place at Cambridge University to become a nurse in London. Furthermore, she is considering withdrawing her evidence, which might mean his name is cleared. Robbie eventually finds a place to sleep overnight but becomes delirious. We later learn that he dies here of septicaemia, and is never reunited with Cecilia.

Part Three returns us to England where Briony is now a nurse at St Thomas' Hospital in London where preparations are fully underway for the arrival of the casualties from France and a possible German invasion. As well as being a nurse, Briony retains her hopes of being a writer and submits a short story – *Two Figures by a Fountain* – to *Horizon* magazine. We discover that it is Part One of *Atonement*. She receives a long letter from its editor, Cyril Connolly, explaining why he has rejected it. Briony learns from her father that Lola and Marshall are to be married in Clapham. It is this information that confirms in her mind that Marshall, not Robbie, raped Lola. After witnessing the ceremony, she walks to meet Cecilia. There is a coldness between them, and the tension increases when Robbie emerges from the bedroom. After an anxious exchange, Briony tells them about the wedding and agrees to write a letter to a solicitor withdrawing her evidence and a long letter to Robbie detailing what she saw that night. The three walk to Balham Underground Station where they say goodbye. We learn in the final part that none of this happened; not only was Robbie dead by this stage, but Cecilia would die at Balham Station during the Blitz.

The fourth section of the novel is set in London in 1999. Briony is a successful author, but she has been diagnosed with a form of dementia which means that her mind will eventually 'shut down'. She has just finished writing her final novel – much of the book that we have just read – and she is in the process of both handing back her research materials to the Imperial War Museum, and preparing for a family dinner held in her honour, at the old Tallis home (which is now a hotel). Before leaving the Museum she sees Lola and Paul (now Lord and Lady Marshall) getting into a car: she is a sprightly woman of nearly 80, but he is frail. Nevertheless, it means that Briony cannot publish what happened, with details of the rape, because it would be libellous. She goes to the dinner and reflects on what really happened to Robbie, Cecilia and other members of her family. The book comes full circle with a performance by various grandchildren of *The Trials of Arabella*. Briony admits that, as an act of atonement, she has rewritten Robbie's and Cecilia's fate, bringing them together in love.

Part/chapter summaries and commentaries

Target your thinking

- What themes and ideas does McEwan explore? (**AO1**)
- How does McEwan use narrative methods to shape the reader's responses as the story develops? (**AO2**)
- In what ways does McEwan present characters and settings? (**AO2**)

Part One

Chapter 1

It is the summer of 1935 and Briony Tallis, a 13-year-old girl, is putting the finishing touches to *The Trials of Arabella*, a short melodrama she has written to celebrate the return of her brother Leon to the family home the next day. The cast will include her cousins – Jackson and Pierrot (twins, aged 9) and Lola (aged 15) who are about to arrive at the Tallis house for an indefinite period while their parents undergo a bitter divorce. We learn in Chapter 2 that their mother, Hermione Quincey, is in Paris with her lover. Briony has great hopes for the play, but they quickly fade once she has met the Quincey children. Physically, they are very different from how she had imagined them. Additionally, the boys do not like plays. In the first meeting to discuss who should play the characters, Briony's script is 'wrecked', and the tension is only relieved when Briony's elder sister, Cecilia, calls the twins for their bath.

Commentary Narrative perspective is an important technique used by McEwan throughout the novel. We see certain events viewed through different eyes, with different perspectives. By doing this McEwan asks us to consider what is true, and what is false. He begins the novel in the third person, with Briony as the focal character: as a result we are invited to see events – as well as the wider world – as she sees it, and, at this stage, to sympathise with her views. But her desire to control – to arrive at certainties marked with 'indispensable' exclamation marks, to prefer glamorous fiction to 'the unglamorous face' of reality – will have disastrous consequences. Yet at this stage it is represented as something innocent.

Many of the key themes in the novel (such as innocence, experience, deception and forgiveness) are introduced in this opening chapter. But perhaps the most important is the difference between appearance and reality, and this is developed with the arrival of Briony's cousins. They do not 'look' like the characters she has created: Briony becomes increasingly frustrated when her script is spoilt as it is read aloud, and she begins to lose control over what she has written.

Chapter 2

The middle child of three, Cecilia Tallis is home from Cambridge University after completing her degree in English Literature. As she refreshes some flowers in the large fountain in the grounds of the house she sees her childhood friend – and contemporary at Cambridge – Robbie Turner in the distance. Not wishing to talk to him, Cecilia goes into the house and, alone in the living room, reflects on her life.

Once indoors she picks a vase for the flowers. But this is no ordinary vase: it was given to her late Uncle Clem by the people of Verdun as he helped liberate the town from German forces in the First World War. Cecilia goes outside to ask Robbie for a cigarette, and during a tense exchange she leans over to dip the vase into the fountain. As Robbie reaches out to help her, she grips the vase until it cracks. Two triangular pieces break off, falling into the water. Cecilia strips to her underwear, slips into the water and retrieves the pieces. After dressing quickly and angrily, Cecilia walks back to the house, leaving Robbie alone.

▲ The breaking of the vase is a pivotal moment for Cecilia, Robbie and Briony

Commentary The narrative perspective shifts again in this chapter as McEwan focuses not only on the relationship between Cecilia and Robbie, but broadens it to place the novel in a wider perspective. The reference to the house being condemned 'one day' in an article subtly suggests that the narrative is retrospective. What might appear on the surface to be a realist, third-person narrative, is actually a fictive narrative written from Briony's perspective. The status of the text is much more uncertain than we might at first realise, and what appears to be a stable world seen from reliable perspectives is actually something much less secure.

Build critical skills

Motifs are repeated elements or symbols that writers use to reinforce and extend particular ideas in a text. Think about how triangles might be used: what could they represent? Now make a note of every mention of a triangle, and also every possible 'triangular' relationship introduced by McEwan.

The breaking of the vase at the fountain is a pivotal moment in the novel. The vase could be symbolic of everything that is fragile and too easily lost: ranging from Cecilia's virginity, to Robbie's freedom, to life itself. Its design can also be seen as symbolic and reflects the gathering of characters in the Tallis household, soon to be shattered. The pieces broken off are triangular. Triangles not only act as a motif in *Atonement*, but relationships are often framed triangularly: for instance, Briony is the third observer of the scene, and this in turn foreshadows her seeing, and misinterpreting, the scene in the library in Chapter 10. Perspective, wilful misinterpretation, false conclusions: all these ideas and more are developed in this chapter and the next.

Chapter 3

Meanwhile, preparations for the play continue to go badly: Briony suspects that Lola is planning to get all the attention, while at the same time allowing her younger brothers to ruin the performance. As they rehearse, Danny Hardman – the son of one of the servants – looks on until asked to leave. Eventually the rehearsals break down, leaving Briony alone; she contemplates reading, writing and identity, finding the act of writing a story comforting, magical even. As she thinks about this and other things, her attention is drawn to what is happening outside her window between Cecilia and Robbie.

Commentary After the action in the second chapter, the third is more reflective. However, McEwan uses this chapter to develop complex ideas about identity and existence, and he does so by shifting the narrative focus back on Briony. She contemplates the nature of truth, asking herself if logic and emotion are equally valid ways of knowing something. Such a theoretical debate soon has practical relevance as Briony watches the incident at the fountain. For her it is an 'illogical' sequence of events which, in another reference to the future, would take years to make sense of (or 'refine'). There is a tension here between what she observes as a young girl and what is added by the adult, decades later. However, she decides that she will try to interpret it through writing about it 'three times over, from three points of view'. She believes that each perspective will have 'equal value'. However, as we shall see, some views, and some interpretations, are truer than others, and her inability to see this, far from being creative, can be very destructive.

Chapter 4

It is now the afternoon and Cecilia encounters an upset Briony in the hallway outside the library. Briony decides against telling her sister what she has just seen happen between her and Robbie, preferring instead to blame her mood on the failure of the play. Cecilia greets her brother and his friend Paul Marshall. We learn that Marshall has made a lot of money out of producing a chocolate bar called Amo. In the first mention of the political events happening in Europe, production of Amos could increase if the British Army starts issuing them to all its soldiers.

Leon tells Cecilia that he has invited Robbie to dinner that evening, which angers her, and she asks Leon to uninvite him but he refuses to do so. The tension between the two is only broken when they decide to go indoors for cocktails, and as they go, Cecilia thinks that Marshall faintly touches her arm.

Commentary With each new viewpoint comes the possibility of greater misunderstanding. No sooner is Cecilia observed by Briony than she becomes the voyeur, 'trespassing' in the guest's room, illicitly watching Robbie as he walks towards the 'trap' that is Leon and Paul Marshall. Voyeurism carries with it a sexual threat, and this is developed with the second mention of Danny Hardman who, again, is an onlooker. His name suggests physical strength (as well as something more overtly sexual); like Lola, he is at the crossroads of innocence and experience. Marshall is staying in Auntie Venus' room (named after a relative who lived there for many years) – Venus is the Roman goddess of desire.

Other references to sex include Cecilia observing that Marshall has 'pubic hair growing from his ears', and she fantasises, 'self-destructively', that should she marry him, he would 'fill her with his big-faced children', something which she finds 'almost erotic'. The sense of ambiguity continues throughout the rest of the chapter, both in how the characters relate to each other and how they view Robbie. The chapter ends with Marshall smiling and allowing Cecilia to go first through a gap in the thicket; as she passes he touches her lightly on the forearm. 'Or it may have been a leaf': once again, perspective and interpretation are all important.

Chapter 5

Briony abandons rehearsals of the play. Left without this project, the Quincey children return to the nursery where they soon begin to argue: they are homesick and hungry, and in one argument Jackson exclaims that they will never be able to return home because of their parents' divorce. This is the first time this word has been used by any of them in public, and it breaks a taboo, leaving them all shocked. However, before the argument develops Paul Marshall enters the room where he talks to the children about his work, as well as their parents. Now sexual tension begins to develop between Lola and Marshall. At the end of the chapter he gives her one of his Amo chocolate bars and urges her to bite into it.

Commentary The Quincey children, who are becoming increasingly lonely, retreat symbolically to the nursery. Jackson's use of the word 'divorce' has the same effect that a swear word might have (it is 'an unthinkable obscenity'), and it foreshadows Robbie's own use of a genuinely obscene word in his letter to Cecilia in Chapter 9. In this novel, individual words are incredibly powerful. By acknowledging the end of their parents' marriage the two figures of authority have quickly been reduced to 'a ruined totem of a lost golden age'. It leaves the children feeling alone, and vulnerable.

At this point, ironically, Paul Marshall, dressed in white enters, but he is no guardian angel. Lola notices his 'cruel face', but instead of reading such signs accurately she find it 'an attractive combination': it fits into a pattern of misreadings and ignored warnings that reoccur throughout the novel, with disastrous effects.

McEwan makes it clear that we are to view Marshall as a figure of questionable morality: he has, after all, just woken from an erotic dream involving his four younger sisters. As he looks at Lola he sees her as 'almost a young woman' (although McEwan's description of her 'narrow hips' reminds us of her youth). He tells her that she reminds him of his favourite sister, but given the dream he has just had, this carries with it a clear sexual charge. Again we have to consider where responsibilities lie. The conflict between appearance and reality is further developed in this chapter: for example, Lola claims that she saw *Hamlet* – a play with adult themes, when in fact she went to the pantomime. Another example can be found in the naming of the 'Amo' chocolate bar: it sounds exactly like 'ammo', the popular abbreviation for 'ammunition', but for Lola it is reminiscent of the 'Amo, Amas, Amat' ('I love, you love, he loves'), which she would probably have recited many times in school. All this is set against a wider context of war and peace: the children claim that war will not happen, but Marshall claims, with real certainty, that it will (and indeed, his business depends on it).

The chapter ends with a heightened sense of sexual charge between Marshall and Lola. She places his chocolate in her mouth, her tongue curling around it, her 'unblemished', virginal white teeth poised, but reluctant to break into it until – after crossing and uncrossing his legs – Marshall demands she bites. As she does so Marshall observes her over the 'steeple he made with his hands', the same gesture, with its connotations of religion and self-confidence, that Cecilia makes in the library, after reading Robbie's obscene letter and before they make love.

Chapter 6

Emily Tallis, 46 years old, wife of Jack and mother of Leon, Cecilia and Briony, is in her bedroom, trying to avoid another of the many migraines that leave her bedridden for much of the novel. As she lies in the dark, she frets about her children. We learn that Leon has refused help from his father to start a career in the civil service and now works in a small private bank. He is 'sweet-natured', handsome, popular, content and completely lacking in ambition. Emily is less patient with Cecilia who, after graduating (we learn later she gained a Third, the lowest class of degree), has yet to find a job, a skill or a husband. It makes her mother cross. Her 'darling' Briony seems to be her mother's favourite. She regrets the inevitable growing up of her children, and this regret is emphasised as she listens to the different sounds that spread throughout the house: the play rehearsal, the twins' bath time and the arrival of the guests. Gradually, the migraine begins to improve and she gets out of bed to face the afternoon.

Taking it further ▶

Why do you think Lola responds in this way? Is McEwan emphasising her innocence, or her yearning for adult pleasure?

Commentary Although this chapter focuses entirely on one character's concerns, with no dialogue or interaction with another character, it does develop key themes and tells us more about some of the main characters. It is a chapter dominated by pain and regret. Emily Tallis is battling a migraine that resembles a 'curled and sleeping animal', a 'lazy creature' that, if provoked, will become a 'caged panther'. Held at 'knife-point', afraid of moving in case it stirs, Emily contemplates her life. Perhaps the pain influences her view of herself and her family, but this is a mother who is disappointed with her two eldest children, and even 'poor' Briony, the 'softest little thing', is described in pitying terms. What makes things worse is that all her children are moving away from her, and at her age she knows there will be no more.

Innocence and experience, and how they intersect, are important ideas in this chapter. McEwan also develops the theme of interpretation (and misinterpretation) through Emily. She believes she knows 'everything', but she actually misunderstands. For example, she interprets Marshall's interest in Lola as innocent, saying to herself that he 'might not be such a bad sort, if he was prepared to pass the time of day entertaining children'. We also learn that Jack, her husband, will have 'forgotten to tell her he was not coming home'. Thus although Emily Tallis sees herself at the centre of the household, knowing everything, she is in fact isolated, lonely and imprisoned by pain. Importantly, for the plot, her belief in being 'fine-tuned' to events is deeply misguided.

Chapter 7

The chapter begins with a detailed description of the island temple. It has not had a happy history: built in the 1780s 'to enhance the pastoral ideal', it has been in decline ever since. It is now in a state of dilapidation. This is the place Briony comes to after the abandonment of her play. She takes out her anger on the nettles that have grown in this neglected part of the grounds. As she thrashes away at them she begins to create a narrative: the plants stand in for Lola and the twins, and eventually her career as a playwright, and then her own childhood. All are destroyed by her. Eventually she is made aware of her brother and Paul Marshall arriving to stay as they are driven down the driveway, and also of them observing her. These thoughts dispel her daydreaming, and she begins the more difficult journey back through the destroyed nettles, then decides to wait on the bridge until someone tries to find her.

Commentary Once again, appearance and reality dominate this chapter. The island temple was conceived to cast 'an interesting reflection on the lake', rather than be interesting itself. Almost everything about it is 'false': it is 'in the style of' Nicholas Revett; although a temple, it has 'no religious purpose at all'. Although it might once have been built to complement the (now destroyed) original house, its meaning has now been lost. What remains cannot be understood by the Tallis family, developing the theme of misinterpretation. The building 'wears its own black band', and it is this sombre note of tragedy that stops the building being completely 'fake'.

Taking it further ▶

Spend time researching Nicholas Revett and neoclassical Georgian architecture. Then, answer these questions:

Why did the aristocracy pay for such buildings to be constructed in their grounds?

Why do you think McEwan has chosen to include such a detailed description of the temple in this chapter?

TASK

McEwan references three of the seven deadly sins in Chapter 7: pride, gluttony and avarice (or greed). What of the other sins – lust, anger and sloth (laziness) – have been evident in the chapters you have read so far? To what extent would you agree that McEwan's novel is a strongly moral tale with each of the characters deserving their fate?

Briony's arrival adds to the atmosphere of death. As she slashes at the nettles, she begins to compose a narrative for her actions: the nettles stand in for Lola, one has its leaves 'turned outwards like hands protesting innocence'. The imagery used by McEwan is shocking: 'her worthless torso' is sent flying; she is 'poisonous', 'scheming', 'spreading rumours'. She is guilty of deadly sins, such as pride, gluttony and avarice, and Briony murders her with relish. This imagery foreshadows later episodes, including the false accusation of Robbie (and Lola's role in the injustice) as well as the chapters set in the Second World War. But the theme of lost innocence is also explored here: Briony has 'no further need for it', and so it is destroyed, as is her career as a playwright.

Or at least they *appear* to be destroyed, because the irony is that this 'daydreaming' is an innocent act of creativity. As we shall see in Chapter 10, Briony's confusion over what she thinks is a mature action, and what is ill-considered and childish, can have terrible consequences. She is at a crossroads, caught between childhood and adolescence. In another subtle instance of foreshadowing, Briony considers the reality of what she has destroyed, and how difficult it is to come back once such damage has been done. It is 'at this moment of return that the loss became evident' but, as we shall see later on, by then it is too late.

Chapter 8

It is now the early evening and Robbie Turner is lying in the bath in his mother's small bungalow, reflecting on the incident at the fountain. He struggles to understand why Cecilia behaved as she did, and he finds it difficult to reconcile this mature young woman with the girl he has known since childhood. For Robbie she has always been 'like a sister, almost invisible'; even though they were both at Cambridge there was never any intimacy between them, only awkwardness. This has suddenly changed. He decides to write Cecilia a letter of apology. However, after drafting a number of attempts he types a sexually explicit letter, which he never intends to send, but which he finds both amusing and exciting. He sets it to one side and, instead, handwrites another letter, explaining his behaviour at the fountain.

As he gets dressed we learn about his modest background: his mother, Grace, has been the Tallis cleaner since Robbie was six years old, when his father, Ernest, walked out of the home. She is also a clairvoyant. Jack Tallis agreed to be Robbie's patron, paying his university fees, both for his degree in English Literature and for him to study medicine. After a brief conversation with his mother, Robbie gets ready for the dinner that Leon has invited him to (in Chapter 4). Unthinkingly, he places the offensive letter to Cecilia in an envelope and leaves the house, thinking about his future. He has a lot of promise: his degree was the best in his year, and he is looking forward to a successful career as a doctor. As he walks to the Tallis house he meets Briony. He asks her to run ahead of him to deliver the letter to her sister, but no sooner has she run ahead than he realises, to his horror, that he has given her the wrong letter. He shouts after her, but it is too late.

Commentary This is a pivotal chapter that has lasting implications for every character. It begins innocently, with Robbie trying to make sense of Cecilia's actions at the fountain. However, the tone soon changes as he begins to think about her body in almost forensic detail. The motif of the triangle occurs again, this time in reference to the 'triangular darkness' barely concealed by her underwear, and the more he thinks about her, the more aroused he becomes. Robbie's interest is clearly sexual, but such is the detail he goes into (it is referred to at one point as 'an advanced stage of fetishising') that we have to question whether his feelings are natural or something less healthy. Not for the first (or last) time in this novel, we see a character trying to make sense of events by writing about them. But the words are poorly expressed (and, worse, eventually misinterpreted). He decides to write something rude for his own amusement. This note, which describes how he wants to 'kiss [Cecilia's] cunt … [and] make love to [her] all day long' is an admission of his true feelings, but one that he could never express publicly.

It is important to remember how 'self-consciously young' Robbie is, and also how filled with hope and potential his life is. McEwan writes that Robbie is motivated by a desire for 'freedom', which becomes bitterly ironic later on in the novel as it is brutally taken away. Like many young people, Robbie is attempting to find a meaning to life and in doing so he calls on different disciplines, each with its own perspective. He has listened to academics from disciplines including literature, science, politics and psychology, but none have provided a definitive answer. He is impatient to start his new adult life, to find his own success. But at the edge of all these desires is something darker: there is the 'self-destructive folly, or sheer bad luck' that can affect anyone; there is the 'puniness … of mankind' when faced with the 'monstrous patterns of fate'. It is a moment of **proleptic irony** because no sooner has he reflected on this than he gives the note to Briony, and in doing so sets in motion a train of events which will, ultimately, lead to his own death.

Chapter 9

Cecilia is undecided about what to wear for the dinner party. She tries on various outfits, but none please her, one making her appear too old, another too young. Her preparations are interrupted by the twins at her door, and after taking them

Taking it further ▶
Review the characterisation of Robbie. Make notes on what we discover prior to this chapter and then in this chapter. What functions does Robbie perform in this novel? To what extent do you find Robbie a sympathetic character?

proleptic irony: when something is foreshadowed and comes to fruition later in the novel.

back to their bedroom Cecilia notices how neglected the boys are. Feeling guilty, she takes them downstairs with her to join her family. In the kitchen, she finds her mother arguing with Betty the cook, about supper. Eventually Cecilia joins her brother outside where they drink and gossip about work and their plans for the future. Briony joins them, and hands Cecilia Robbie's letter. As Cecilia reads Robbie's words, trying to make sense of them, they are joined by Emily Tallis and Paul Marshall. Cecilia asks her sister if she has read Robbie's letter but does not get a reply.

Commentary As Robbie approaches the Tallis household filled with optimism about his career to come, Cecilia is contemplating her own identity. She looks into the stairway mirror and sees different reflections of herself, ranging from an 'austere, joyless widow' to 'a child of fifteen years before'. She is interrupted by the twins, neglected by everyone now (including their sister) which reminds her of how 'hopeless and terrifying it was … to be without love', and it is this which persuades her to take them downstairs to join the rest of the adults as they prepare for dinner.

The kitchen is described in terms reminiscent of war: 'faces hung at different heights'; there is a 'blurred red' fire; onomatopoeic words describe the noise ('clang', 'clatter'); faces float free, ghost-like, 'their expressions solemn'. This is a place of heat, of meat, of 'heroic, forgotten labours', of tea towels resembling 'decaying regimental banners'. Betty complains that they have been here 'all day in temperatures above the boiling point of *blood*'. It is a skilful anticipation of the forthcoming chapters set in France.

However, sex is also in evidence: Hardman stares at Cecilia until she returns the stare 'fiercely', and is foregrounded still further, this time with a very different response, when Briony hands Robbie's letter to her sister. His words deliver to her an epiphany in which 'everything is explained', including her behaviour towards him. When she asks Briony if she has read the letter it is clear that for both sisters another layer of innocence has peeled away.

Chapter 10

Briony tries to absorb what she has just read in Robbie's letter. However, instead of seeing it as something that might be welcomed by Cecilia, she sees it as a threatening act from which she must protect her sister. In responding in this way, she reveals her lack of awareness. She considers writing something about what she has experienced, but is unsure about how to start. Like Robbie in the previous chapter, the words do not come. Lola joins Briony, clearly upset, she tells her that the twins have attacked her and shows her red marks around her wrist and a scratch on her back. Briony tells Lola about the letter she has just read, and Lola immediately says that Robbie must be reported to the police because he is a 'maniac'. Lola seems to want to confess something to Briony but decides against it. She then leaves to apply make-up. Briony goes to dinner and as she passes the library she notices that, unusually, the door is closed.

On entering the dark room she sees her sister and Robbie making love against the bookshelves. Almost immediately, Cecilia sees Briony, and, horrified, pulls away from Robbie before quickly leaving the room. For a moment Robbie and Briony are left alone, but he keeps his eyes cast downwards and Briony backs out of the library to search for her sister.

Commentary The opening sentence of this important chapter is crucial: Briony is aware that she is 'entering an arena of adult emotion and dissembling'; this is certainly true, but the second half of the sentence, in which she believes that her 'writing was bound to benefit' shows how much growing up she still has to do. She still thinks about herself, and at the cost to others. Robbie's use of the offensive word in his letter disgusts Briony, who simply cannot absorb its full implications: she tries to think of innocuous words that sound like it, and in doing so remove it of its potency, but this fails. Such thoughts increasingly move her to realise that 'it was a chilly sensation, growing up'. Lola's entrance at this point reiterates just how complex this process can be, and how soon we can inhabit the adult world of dissembling. She claims that the marks on her wrists and back have been inflicted by her twin brothers, and Briony believes her, but McEwan subtly suggests something more carnal: Lola dress is 'restrictive', her hair 'loose', her perfume has 'a womanly twang', her voice is 'husky'. Even Lola's interest in Robbie's letter seems prurient (she asks, in a 'hoarse whisper', about him 'thinking about [sex] *all the time*?')

Perhaps speaking from personal experience, it is Lola who describes Robbie as a 'maniac', which Briony misunderstands, seeing it as a 'condition' with 'the weight of medical diagnosis'. Lola clearly knows something more than she is prepared to say, but in this chapter we are closer to Briony's perspective than hers, and this closeness is retained when she discovers Robbie and Cecilia making love. McEwan describes Briony as 'terrified' when her eyes meet her sister's, and of course from a certain perspective sex can look like an assault, rather than something desired; facial expressions can suggest pain rather than pleasure. Robbie looks 'huge and wild' to Briony, Cecilia 'thin' and 'frail'. The response from the adults tells the adult reader everything: there is 'no sign in Cecilia of gratitude or relief', nor is there anything resembling maniacal behaviour from Robbie (instead he 'faced the corner' unable to meet her eyes). Briony misreads all of this, with far-reaching consequences.

Chapter 11

The Tallis family and guests assemble for supper. The atmosphere is hot, claustrophobic and tense. After silence and small talk, the conversation turns to how the heat encourages 'loose morals'. Sharp exchanges follow between the twins and Briony. Robbie thinks about his recent sexual encounter with Cecilia. It is of huge significance to him, but Briony's interruption also causes him to hate someone for the first time.

His reverie is dispelled by the arguments. When Briony accuses the twins of stealing her socks, Cecilia calls her a 'tiresome little prima donna'. The twins leave to go to the lavatory and the focus shifts to Lola and the injuries that, according to Lola and Marshall, the twins have inflicted. As concern for Lola increases, Marshall acts increasingly suspiciously. Briony finds a letter from the twins telling everyone that they have run away. The search for the twins commences. Robbie is the last to leave and, crucially, he does so alone.

Commentary Much of the novel is concerned with the movement between different states – innocence and guilt, youth and age, life and death, war and peace, and even France and England. This chapter represents the 'transitional space' between the old certainties of life before Robbie is accused of rape, and the more chaotic world afterwards. Briony occupies a space 'between the nursery and adult worlds', but she is not alone. When Cecilia and Robbie made love in the library 'they felt watched by their bemused childhood selves' and the motif of the missing child becomes real when the twins run away. Lola is also in a transitional stage, but this is perhaps forced upon her by Marshall.

Everything about this chapter seems intended to make us feel uncomfortable. The atmosphere in the dining room is suffocating: appetites have 'cloyed', the characters are 'nauseated by the prospect of a roast dinner'. It is hot, and there is no water, only sweet, warm wine. The 'dark-stained' panelling adds to the oppressive mood. Conversation is awkward, with tempers frayed. Sex, which is such an important theme in the novel, features strongly here (even the book recalled by Robbie – *Lady Chatterley's Lover* – is an illicit purchase from Soho, an area of London known for its sex trade). Emily Tallis unconsciously comments on recent events when she says that 'hot weather encourage[s] loose morals among young people'; Leon also unconsciously makes a perceptive point about recent events when he states that during a heatwave 'England … is a different country. All the rules change.'

Build critical skills

When Robbie arrives at the Tallis home before his sexual encounter with Cecilia, he notices a 'faithful moth'. To what extent is McEwan drawing a parallel between Robbie and the moth? What might they both symbolise at this stage of the novel?

Context

Lady Chatterley's Lover (1928) by D.H. Lawrence was banned in the United Kingdom until 1960. The novel tells of the love affair between Lady Chatterley and her gamekeeper, Oliver Mellors. For the establishment, the transgression between classes was shocking enough, but Lawrence's explicit language describing sex ensured that it could only be bought illegally (as Robbie did, 'under the counter').

McEwan foreshadows disaster with subtle symbols of death: the painting overlooking them as they eat is of an anonymous family, all as 'pale as ghouls'.

For Robbie, with his 'still-thudding heart', his encounter with Cecilia is a moment of 'transformation' – one which he recounts to himself in intense detail. But sex is not always associated with pleasure. Robbie's excitement is 'close to pain';

the couple 'gnaw' at each other, and Cecilia bites him on the cheek 'not quite playfully'; at times the pain is 'unbearable'. Though painful, their love-making is consensual. A more violent sexual act appears to have occurred between Lola and Marshall.

Taking it further ▷▷

The twins' letter is the second significant letter in the novel; again, it is Briony who delivers it. As you read through the text, note each example of written communication – such as a letter, postcard or note – that is passed between characters. Note also instances of undelivered or misinterpreted items. In what ways are such writings important to McEwan? Consider plot, theme and other areas you think are important.

Chapter 12

After some indecision, Emily Tallis decides not to ask the local police to become involved in the search for the missing twins. Thinking about the children leads her to spend 30 minutes considering a number of things, including her difficult relationship with her sister, Hermione. She sees similarities between her and Lola (most obviously that they are both attention-seekers). Her personal unhappiness is not helped by the distant relationship she has with Jack, who spends much of his time in London working at the Ministry of Defence. Ironically, given his job, theirs is a relationship built on the avoidance of conflict; it is also characterised by deceit. Yet there a pattern to their lives, including the evening telephone calls in which they exchange pleasantries. When Jack does telephone her, later than usual, they talk briefly about various things, including funding Robbie's studies. Emily tells him about the missing twins and Jack decides to ring the police. But their conversation is interrupted by Leon, returning with Cecilia, Briony and a distraught Lola. Leon tells his father to come home because something serious has happened.

Commentary This chapter introduces a more introspective tone, but it is a calm before a storm. McEwan focuses on Emily Tallis and her difficult relationships with other members of her family. Absence seems to link many of the characters she thinks about: her sister, Hermione, is in Paris; Hermione's daughter, Lola, is searching for the missing twins; her husband, Jack, prefers to stay in London than see his family. She is even aware of her ten-year-old self, gone forever, a 'ghost' now 'haunting Emily once more'. The 'fabricated misfortune' that Emily sees in both Lola and Hermione may be inaccurate, but it does foreshadow what happens later in the novel. However, such insights by Emily are not consistent and McEwan emphasises how much Emily listens, but either mishears or misinterprets. For her the missing twins are all a 'drama about nothing'; she even misreads the scale of the war preparations her husband is involved in, preferring instead to see such things as 'silly'.

Context

British rearmament began in earnest in 1934, as a response to the growing threat from Adolf Hitler who came to power in 1933. Before the outbreak of war in 1939, Britain's armed forces grew not only in size, but also in sophistication and effect- iveness. The capacity to destroy whole cities, although difficult to comprehend for Emily, was no exaggeration.

Such misjudgements are contrasted by her husband's decisiveness when he decides to call the police about the missing boys, and Leon's quick and firm response to the unfolding crisis. By the end of the chapter we can see Emily Tallis as an outsider, guided from room to room 'helplessly' by others. She seems ill-prepared to cope with the news that Leon is about to break. In that sense, she is not alone.

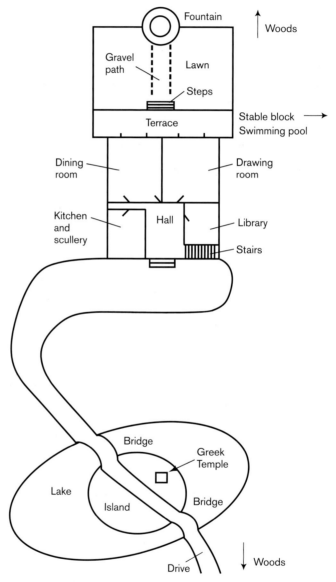

▲ The Tallis house and grounds

Chapter 13

The search for the twins continues. Briony, searching alone in the dark, is caught up in her own thoughts. She thinks about Robbie and realises that this is the first time she has been hated by an adult. This makes her feel more grown up. Her search takes her past the fountain (where the troubles started) and then to the house. She sees her mother, alone, and for a moment considers abandoning the search to cuddle her instead. But she carries on, heading down towards the temple.

Suddenly she sees two figures: one is backing away while the other – Lola – is on the ground. Briony immediately concludes that she has been attacked. They are joined by Leon who picks Lola up to take her back to the house. As they walk Briony begins to tell him what she believes she saw.

Commentary The chapter begins with a striking sentence:

> Within the half hour Briony would commit her crime.

> **Top ten quotation**

This clearly indicates the seriousness of what she is about to do. Her crime is to persuade Lola that she has been 'violated' by Robbie, even though she has no evidence for this. Her interpretation of the scene she stumbles across proves to be the most disastrous misreading of the novel.

Before she finds Lola, Briony embarks on two journeys: one to find the twins, and another – more emotional and psychological – that makes her reassess herself. The second journey explains her behaviour for the rest of this chapter and the next. Her recent experiences – including being hated by Robbie – force her to conclude that there has been 'a moment of coming into being'. In other words, 'her childhood had ended'. She acts as she does because she thinks she is no longer a child. It is a fatal misjudgement.

McEwan develops the idea that much of the action is a sequence of signs to be read. Briony turns events into a narrative but she lacks the maturity to decipher it accurately: although she believes that 'there was nothing she could not describe', the reality is that she is incapable of describing what matters.

She has seen 'an unspeakable word'; the fountain 'foretold of later brutalities'; her mother's mouth 'is easily mistaken for the sign – the hieroglyph – of reproach'. All of these mistaken signs contribute to a 'richer story' which she has to prove herself 'worthy' of writing, but she misunderstands them all. Every crime story must have a villain and Briony has created one in Robbie and is able to fit him into her narrative as soon as she discovers Lola.

The shift in narrative perspective – from the present day to the future – reminds us again that these events are being viewed retrospectively. We can therefore evaluate the consequences of Briony's 'crime'. We are given the benefit of hindsight which makes her actions indefensible.

> She would never be able to console herself that she was pressured or bullied. She never was.

> **Top ten quotation**

It is only when we fully understand her motives, and the choices she takes (and rejects) that we can really see her action as a crime.

Chapter 14

The final chapter of Part One of the novel describes the questioning that follows Briony's 'crime'. The police begin to arrive, including two inspectors, and Dr McLaren (who has come to examine Lola). Marshall arrives soon after and quickly establishes a rapport with the inspectors, sharing cigarettes with them on the terrace. Emily Tallis, unusually, rises to the challenge of the evening, discussing events rather than retreating to her room. In contrast, Cecilia seems agitated, 'always smoking', and on the margins of conversations. Because the twins – and Robbie – are still missing, maps of the estate are consulted. Briony remembers Robbie's letter and runs to give it to a constable. It is handed around, but not commented on until Emily reads it. Cecilia is outraged by their reading of the letter and storms out of the room. The police interview Briony, Emily, Leon, the Hardmans and Marshall (Cecilia refuses to leave her room). Just before 5 a.m. word goes round that Robbie is approaching the house, walking towards them with one of the twins on his shoulder, the other by his side. He is met by the police. Just over an hour later Briony watches from her window as a handcuffed Robbie is led away by police, but not before saying goodbye to Cecilia. As he is driven away his mother, Grace Turner, stops the police car, banging on its bonnet with her umbrella. She is led away, but calls out 'Liars! Liars!' as she watches the car disappear into the distance.

Commentary Again, we are viewing the events in this chapter retrospectively. But McEwan does not remain fixed in one narrative viewpoint: there are references to the 'courtroom from which [Briony's] youth excluded her', and the 'fragmented recollection' of the night in the 'years to come'. A very alert reader will begin to be confirmed in their views that this text is not a realist narrative, but something more complex. The result of this is to stress the importance of what we read: the consequences of each character's actions in this chapter will shape their lives.

Throughout this chapter we witness the adult world gradually making itself more known to Briony: the ease with which Marshall talks to the police, offering them cigarettes from his 'gold case', the 'unmoving mask' of the senior inspector, the hushed tones, the 'manly' consultations between Leon and the doctor – all these details and more are, to Briony, 'at one with her new maturity'. She is the main protagonist but our view of her is ambiguous: it is her 'vile excitement' that adds momentum to the police's enquiries. It is also her description of what she believes she has seen that brings the police to the house, and it is her second delivery of Robbie's letter to the adults that injects a fresh energy, and deeper seriousness, into the investigation. It is Briony who sees the returning Robbie not as someone who has found the missing twins, but as a giant 'seven or eight feet high'. Once again, her view of herself, and her ability to read a situation, is revealed to be misguided and childlike.

Build critical skills

How 'evil' is Briony? McEwan writes that she realises that 'evil was complicated and misleading', but is her crime, compounded by the actions she takes in this chapter, evil? How would you define this word, and do you think children are capable of committing evil? Should we distinguish between the sin and the sinner? Think about such distinctions as you explore the novel.

Build critical skills

Grace Turner's first name has, like the title of the novel, strong associations with spirituality. Look this word up: why do you think McEwan has chosen this name for this character?

The misreadings continue: Robbie, who should have been welcomed as a returning hero for finding the twins, is arrested and driven away by police. And in her second witnessing of intimacy between Robbie and Cecilia, Briony wrongly interprets her sister's actions as 'forgiveness', an act of atonement (for an act he is innocent of) rather than gestures of tenderness and love. Had the chapter ended with Briony's mistaken view of events we might have lost sight of the injustice of what has just happened. Instead, it is left to Robbie's mother, Grace, to state unambiguously that all those assembled are 'Liars! Liars!' and that each have contributed to the framing of an innocent man.

Part Two

Five years have passed, and we are now in northern France in 1940. Robbie Turner – a private in the British Expeditionary Force (BEF) and two corporals (Nettle and Mace) – have been walking for several days to Dunkirk to join the evacuation of Allied soldiers. Although Robbie is the lowest in rank, the other men defer to him: he has a map, is fluent in French and, importantly, he speaks 'like a toff'.

Death and destruction are everywhere. The men discover a bombed-out house and, in a moment of the absurd, notice a human leg (Robbie speculates to himself that it could be a child's) wedged 20 feet up in a tree. The leg is a 'haunting detail', but its real power lies in conveying the random brutality of war.

Taking it further ▶

What examples of grace – in its different interpretations – can be found in Part One of the novel? Explain their importance.

> ## CRITICAL VIEW
>
> The novelist Martin Amis, when asked what he considered to be McEwan's greatest achievement, said, 'the first two hundred pages of *Atonement*'. To what extent would you agree with this view?

> ## Context
>
> ```
> The evacuation of Allied forces from Dunkirk occurred
> between 27 May and 4 June 1940. A flotilla of 900 naval and
> civilian crafts rescued 338,226 people from the beaches;
> throughout, the German airforce - the Luftwaffe - attacked,
> destroying Dunkirk and the surrounding area, killing at
> least 5,000 soldiers. Many civilians also died. Over one
> million Allied soldiers were taken prisoner by the Germans.
> Historical opinion remains divided about the impact Dunkirk
> had on the British campaign: the British Prime Minister,
> Winston Churchill, described it as a 'colossal military
> disaster', a humiliating retreat; but there is also a view
> that the nation's morale was given an important boost.
> ```

Robbie has some shrapnel just below his rib cage and his wound is getting worse, draining his energy. But they walk on, aware of the battles (the 'vast upheavals') going on in the distance. They are met at a farm by an elderly woman who tries to scare them off, claiming her sons will kill them on their return. Undeterred, the three British soldiers move to her barn to rest.

Evening descends and eventually the two sons – Henri and Jean-Marie Bonnet – return. They are kindly men in their 50s, willing to share their food and wine. We learn that they have travelled from Arras, the scene of a battle. The conversation turns to the Allied retreat, and Robbie promises to return to 'throw' the Germans out of France.

As Robbie tries to sleep he thinks of his three-and-a-half years in jail. He negotiated an early release so that he could join the infantry; Cecilia has promised to wait for him. They have corresponded throughout his time in Wandsworth prison, writing in a private language so that their letters escape being censored. Robbie's only visitor in prison has been his mother.

He visits the memory of being released from jail in 1939 and arranging to meet Cecilia in London. She has become a nurse in a maternity hospital and has cut herself off from her family because of their behaviour over his conviction. Compared to prison, Robbie finds military training not unenjoyable. They walk to catch a bus and before they part they kiss, at first tentatively, and then with passion.

War casts its shadow across their lives: he is eventually sent to northern France and she has to train to deal with severe trauma injuries in Liverpool. But they continue to write and each of her letters concludes with the same words she whispered to him before he was taken away in the police car:

Top ten quotation

I'll wait for you. Come back.

In one letter Cecilia tells him that Briony is beginning to understand the seriousness of her 'crime'. Perhaps in an act of penance, she has decided not to go to Cambridge University but, like Cecilia, train to be a nurse. She is also exploring whether she can change her evidence, which might mean that Robbie's conviction is overturned.

At dawn Robbie is awoken after a brief sleep. The three men carry on walking, watching the German bombers heading for the coast and listening to the Allied artillery fire. They are 25 miles from Dunkirk and Robbie's injury is beginning to worsen. The closer they get to the coast, the more the traffic increases, and the more at risk from German fire they become. The three men merge with the mix of families and soldiers fleeing from the German troops. Amid the chaos, Robbie witnesses many violent and disturbing scenes. At one point Robbie, Nettle and Mace are stopped by a major who demands that they join him in attacking some German soldiers in the woods, but before this develops a German fighter plane flies low over the crowds, firing at will. Robbie shelters behind an overturned lorry, narrowly avoiding being hit.

The longer that Robbie has to walk, the more he begins to think about his own life, and the life that he could have if Briony withdraws her evidence. Although he tries to think calmly about this happening, promising himself that he would 'simply resume' and apply to medical college, clearing his name is hugely important to him. But in order to do this he has to try to forgive Briony, which is not something he can easily do. He tells himself 'over and over again':

Yes, she was just a child. But not every child sends a man to prison with a lie. Not every child is so purposeful and malign, so consistent over time, never wavering, never doubted.

Top ten quotation

In trying to understand Briony's motives, Robbie recalls a moment from 1932. He had started to teach her how to swim, and they used the river near the Tallis home for these lessons. Briony was then about ten years old; Robbie had not yet gone up to Cambridge. During one of these lessons Briony had jumped in and Robbie had to save her. She did so because she wanted to prove how she loved him, and also to see if this was reciprocated. She confesses to him that she loves him. He dismissed it then but now, in the light of his conviction, cannot easily forget.

Robbie's reflections are broken by the confusion around him, and by another rescue. He moves a boy and his mother from being killed by a Stuka bomb, before another bomb lands, 'vaporising' them and sending Robbie several feet into the air. He makes it to the shelter of the woods where he is reunited with Mace and Nettle. They march, but by now the wound hurts Robbie with every step. They make it to the beach where they see 'ten, twenty thousand, perhaps more' waiting to be rescued. But there are no ships to be seen, and so the three men move to the ransacked resort where other soldiers wait. They witness an ugly scene between British soldiers and a solitary RAF man: the Tommies blame him for the lack of air cover, but just before he is attacked by the crowd Mace picks him up and rescues him.

▲ The horrors of Dunkirk

Nettle and Robbie move on and, as a reward for capturing an old woman's pig, are given water, wine, some sausage and sugared almonds. But by now Robbie seems to be making less and less sense to Nettle, and it is with difficulty that they find a cellar, crammed with other British soldiers, where the atmosphere is one of exhaustion and threat. Robbie soon begins to fall into a restless sleep, dreaming of the images he has seen during the last few days mingled with his love of Cecilia. He begins to cry out, causing Nettle to tell him to be quiet, and it is now that his companion notices how feverish Robbie has become. He is dangerously ill and hallucinating, and as he begins to fall asleep again his last thoughts are of Cecilia. 'You won't hear another word from me' he promises, and they are, indeed, Robbie's last words.

Commentary Part Two is dominated by being saved: and this extends from the purely physical rescue from Dunkirk, to being saved by love and forgiveness.

The three men – Robbie, Nettle and Mace – are searching for a way back to England. Their journey takes them through a French countryside devastated by war. These pages have an atmosphere that moves between hope and despair, and these emotions are framed by death. There are images bordering on the surreal, but which also develop familiar themes. For example, the leg that Robbie sees in the tree is both horrific and surreal, and takes on greater significance by the end of the part. This death also adds to the growing list of missing – or absent – people we read about in the novel (including, in this part, Paul Bonnet).

Taking it further ▶

Think about how many characters in the novel have either gone missing (and been found), are lost, cut themselves off from others, or are absent for much of the narrative. This is a recurrent theme in McEwan's writing (one of his novels, *The Child in Time*, is concerned with a missing girl). Why is it so important to this novel? What does it signify?

Taking it further ▶

The swarm of bees that McEwan describes is immediately compared to the war effort ('general conscription!'). How does this explicitly figurative writing add to the narrative? To what extent do you think such techniques are consistent with the rest of the novel?

If we have seen an injustice done to Robbie in the previous section of the novel, we see many more now, and they are on an epic scale. We are witnessing the projected figures written out by Jack Tallis in Chapter 12 made real: it is 'an industrial process'.

Death, and the need to be rescued from it, forces the three men to continue their walk towards Dunkirk. It is a journey with moving depictions of how the war has affected others: the Bonnet brothers' account of Arras and their brother's death captures the extent of the war, but is also intimate: amid all these acts of casual cruelty these British and French men show kindness to each other. Perhaps it is because death is so close that Robbie contemplates his own fate in such depth throughout this section. The story of his ongoing love affair with Cecilia is subtly revealed: it is fragile, but able to endure his three-and-a-half years in prison. Her love rescues him, allowing him to retain some hope.

TASK

Note which different time periods are narrated through Robbie. In what ways do these shifting perspectives add to the reader's understanding of:
- Robbie
- other characters
- themes?

Yet that hope for the future can only grow if Briony withdraws her evidence against him. For Robbie,

Top ten quotation ▷

> to be cleared would be a pure state. He dreamed of it like a lover, with a simple longing.

For this to happen, Briony would have to 'recant' and carry out an act of 'absolution' – phrases that, like atonement, have strong religious connotations. If she 'saves' Robbie she also 'saves' herself, and she will do so because 'her conscience could no longer bear' the crime she had committed. But it would be a reciprocated act of salvation because we learn that Robbie saved her from drowning when she was a child. Crucially, though, Robbie

> did not forgive her. He would never forgive her. That was the lasting damage.

Build critical skills

How important do you think forgiveness is in this novel? Robbie's unwillingness to forgive Briony is described as a 'lasting damage'. Do you think McEwan's novel has a strong moral purpose, asking us to learn to forgive, to seek atonement for our crimes in return? To what extent does the ability to forgive – or not – determine the fates of the novel's characters?

The conflict is not just between the Allies and the German forces but also between order and chaos. The pages describing the journey to the beach articulate what happens when social structures begin to break down: on the surface, normality continues as women buy shoes for their children and men walk their dogs, but 'parallel' to this Robbie sees a mother and son 'vaporised' by a German bomb, soldiers and civilians killed on an 'industrial' scale. The military hierarchy is also challenged as soldiers desperately try to stay alive: the major who commands Robbie to join him to fight 'Jerry' is mocked by Nettle. The normal rules of society – which we saw inverted in Part One by the weather, and people's behaviour – are tested still further here.

McEwan fills these pages with small but telling episodes because 'without the details there could be no larger picture', and each contributes to the multilayered narrative. Robbie is devising 'his own story' as he walks, and even taps out its own 'rhythm', a **hexameter** of five **iambs** (or **feet**) and 'an **anapaest**'. For Robbie 'his words were bringing it into being', but, as we have seen in Part One, with such creation comes the suggestion of fiction, deception and, another familiar theme in the novel, misinterpretation.

> ## TASK
> Five sugared almonds are traditionally given at weddings: their bittersweet taste can represent life's ups and downs, and they individually symbolise health, wealth, happiness, children and a long life. Shortly before he dies Robbie eats a sugared almond, 'whose sweetness belonged to another world'. Think about the symbolism of this moment: how does it affect our reading of these final pages, and the text as a whole?

The 'dreamlike' atmosphere of the narrative threatens to become a 'nightmare' as Robbie's injury worsens. Images of death become more prominent: at one stage Nettle and Mace are 'in the final stages of digging a grave … sing[ing] tunelessly for Turner's benefit'.

As Robbie begins to fall asleep there is a long passage of extraordinary power which brings together key themes and symbols: it is momentarily interrupted by Corporal Nettle, who reminds us not only of how ill Robbie is, but how close to being rescued they are. But it is too late for Robbie: his final moments are 'calm', filled with the familiar refrain with which Cecilia signs off every letter. Her words are 'elemental', as are his last memories, of sight ('the green dress'), sound ('Come back'), and touch ('the icy touch of the handcuffs'). There will be no 'rushing the boats' for Robbie: the seas that await him are the tranquil waters of death.

Part Three

While Robbie is waiting to be rescued from Dunkirk, Briony Tallis is learning the craft of nursing at St Thomas' Hospital in London. She writes home regularly, and in return finds out what is happening to the old household. The fountain has been broken by one of the evacuees posted there, and Betty has dropped Uncle Clem's vase, smashing it to pieces. Briony has written a story and submitted it to *Horizon* magazine. In a letter from her father, we learn that Paul Marshall and Lola Quincey are to be married.

Briony has to suddenly deal with the wounded arriving from Dunkirk. She does well and gains the respect of the formidable Sister Drummond. The soldiers surprise her: some are very brave – even joking about their injuries – others cry 'like giant babies'. One young French man stands out. He engages her in a rambling conversation and at first she tries to keep him to the facts. But then she realises he is dying, and so when, in his delirious state, he asks her if she loves him she says 'yes' because 'no other reply was possible'. In a matter of hours she learns everything she needed to know about nursing.

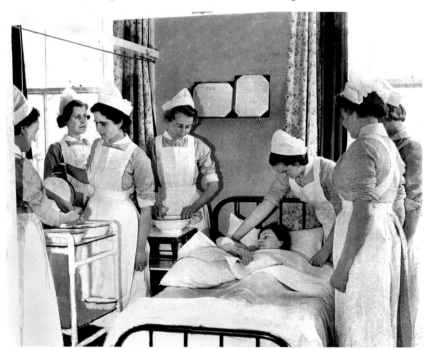

▲ Hospitals during the war were run with military precision

Briony receives a reply from Cyril Connolly, the editor of *Horizon* magazine. It is perhaps the key letter in *Atonement* because, unlike Robbie's to Cecilia, it profoundly alters how we as readers view the novel. Connolly analyses her story, *Two Figures by a Fountain*. It is the story of Robbie and Cecilia. We realise that some – if not all – of what we have read is a fiction created by Briony Tallis. In a pastiche of Connolly's own writing style, McEwan deconstructs Part One of his own novel, exposing its lack of action as deliberate – a poor imitation of Virginia Woolf's technique.

After this critical interlude, we return to the action of wartime London. Preparations continue for a German attack on the capital but Briony has her mind set on more domestic concerns. She goes to the wedding of Lola and Marshall. She decides against interrupting the service and watches them drive away in a black Rolls Royce.

Briony walks to her sister's house in Balham. They have not seen each other for years, but she gets an unfriendly reception. Cecilia is working at an Emergency Medical Services hospital, bearing 'the real brunt of the evacuation'. Briony notices that her elder sister has aged well, and is now 'boldly sensual'. After some small talk about their family (including the news that young Hardman died serving in the Royal Navy), the sisters discuss Briony's 'crime'.

At this point Robbie enters from the bedroom. He is furious with Briony, asking her if she knows what it is like to be in jail. Briony tells them that young Hardman did not rape Lola: it was Marshall, and she has just come from their wedding. The news stuns them both. Eventually they decide on a plan of action: Briony will go to a solicitor and make a statement retracting her evidence; she will then write a long letter to Robbie telling him everything she knows about the case. Once this is agreed they walk to Balham tube station and, before they say goodbye, Briony apologises for what she has done.

Commentary This part profoundly alters the reader's view of the novel. For some it is a highly accomplished piece of postmodern fiction that challenges our assumptions about characterisation and plot; for others it undermines not just the integrity of this novel, but of the writer's relationship with his reader. The nexus of this conflict is Cyril Connolly's rejection of Briony's story, *Two Figures by a Fountain*.

Much of the action in Part Three happens at the same time as Part Two, but the focus now is on Briony, not Robbie. We have also moved from France back to England. Furthermore, we have gone from what is a very male environment (the army) to a very female environment (nursing).

We have also moved from those who are waiting to be saved, to those who must do the saving. Much of the nurses' time is spent waiting for the inevitable casualties that will come from France. McEwan vividly describes what it was like to work on a hospital ward at the time: the routine, the indifference to personal issues, and above all the 'languorous' waiting. However, the 'unease that was out there in the streets' is, for Briony, not just the prospect of invasion, but also something more private.

The past remains present. When Briony tries to speak to her father from a telephone box, all she hears is a nasal voice repeatedly saying, 'Trying to connect you' before the connection is 'broken', finally going dead.

> It was still an innocent time … The dead were not yet present, the absent were presumed alive. The scene was dreamlike in its normality.

The letters from home remind her of how things have changed, but also how connected they are with the past: the fountain has been damaged by a young

Build critical skills

McEwan writes that 'the model behind [nursing] …was military'. What are the main similarities and differences between Robbie's life in the British Army and Briony's life in St Thomas' Hospital?

Top ten quotation

Taking it further ▶

To what extent do you think that this is a book concerned with the past's relationship with the present day? How might McEwan be claiming that we can never escape the consequences of our past actions?

child, and Uncle Clem's vase has been completely destroyed because 'the pieces had simply come away' in Betty's hands (a result of Cecilia's earlier flawed repairs). Cecilia and Robbie, although absent – and silent – remain in her thoughts. Even Fiona (Briony's new friend) reminds her of Lola.

It is Lola – now 20 – who we see again in this part marrying Paul Marshall (nine years her senior). Briony's motive for attending the wedding is easy to understand now: she is in every sense the author of their fates because she 'had made it possible'. And she continues to make the connections between Robbie and Cecilia, aware of the 'secret torment' that was her crime, and the fear that Robbie will not return to Cecilia. After reading Connolly's letter we realise she has the power to ensure that he *will* appear again, 'rubbed with a blunt pencil', like an image from a children's book. They will be reunited, if not in the flesh, then on the page. This is why she continues to write: 'it is the only place she could be free', and it is the only place where she can establish her own 'rules'.

> The evasions of her little novel were exactly those of her life. Everything she did not wish to confront was also missing from her novella – and was necessary to it.

The rules she has to learn to be a nurse are ignored by the 'wild race of men from a terrible world'. This world reveals 'every secret of the body', and what should remain concealed – bone, optic nerves – rise up through the flesh. It is, for Briony, 'sacrilegious'. What she has to do is create another world, where she is God, controlling others' fates. For Briony, the author and the nurse, a softer fantasy world where connections can be constructed and maintained through words is worthy of creation. So, the young Frenchman dies believing that Briony loves him: although a lie, this is far preferable to Robbie's fate.

Taking it further ▶

Read Geoff Dyer's critical view carefully. What would your answer be to each question? In the light of the questions, what have you learnt of Briony's characterisation, and ideas of atonement in the novel?

Writer and critic Geoff Dyer has written about this section of the novel:

> *Does this devotion to the victims of war wash her hands of her earlier guilt? Does her atonement depend on Robbie's survival? Or can it be achieved through the eventual realization of her literary ambitions – through a novel such as the one we are reading? Who can grant atonement to the novelist, whose God-like capacity to create and rework the world means that there is no higher authority to whom appeal can be made?*

But all fiction is a lie, and we see this no more clearly than in Briony's rejection letter. Here Part One of *Atonement* is deconstructed by a 'real' critic (who is, of course, McEwan). The possible weaknesses we might have been aware of when reading Part One – the lack of pace, the many misinterpretations – are singled out for analysis. Connolly writes:

The crystalline present moment is of course a worthy subject in itself … However, such writing can become precious when there is no sense of forward movement.

Top ten quotation

Context

```
Briony's story is criticised as being too derivative of
Virginia Woolf (1882-1941). Woolf was a very influential
novelist during the interwar years: her books inspired
many women to write, and to become feminists. Her style is
intensely poetic, putting her characters' emotional states
over plot development.
```

Taking it further ▶▶

Connolly also makes reference to two other writers. The unlikeliness of a relationship between Cecilia and Robbie is an allusion to *Lady Chatterley's Lover* by D.H. Lawrence (1885–1930). 'Dusty Answer' by Rosamond Lehmann, published in 1927, is also referred to. Why do you think McEwan wants us to think specifically about these two texts?

Taking it further ▶

After reading Connolly's letter, to what extent would you agree with his criticisms of Part One of the novel? How valid are his points? Do you think that these deliberate imperfections in the text actually strengthen the novel or weaken it?

His letter is referred to as a 'sugar-coated rejection slip' (which is reminiscent not only of Robbie's sugared almonds, but also Marshall's Amo bars that litter France, and develop the theme of appearance and reality). But the novel does gain forward movement in Parts Two and Three as the central characters both travel to a point where they might be saved. However, after reading Connolly's letter we have to ask if this was only possible *because* of his words.

Briony's journeying – like Robbie's – is both emotional and physical: she grows up in these pages, but she also walks for miles (again, like Robbie, carrying an injury), observing the details of life around her, before arriving at Lola's wedding. As with Robbie, what might appear to be an appointment with love is something closer to death (Lola and Marshall are described as being 'walled up within the mausoleum of their marriage'). And also like Robbie, the whole experience is deeply ambiguous, even more so after reading Connolly's letter.

Once again, Briony is reminded of the connections between the past and the present, and how the lies told on one evening have resulted in a rape victim marrying her rapist. These connections spread outwards, like the streets that link Clapham to Balham; they also turn inwards, tying different parts of the text together. Now that we are aware of the novel's intricate construction, McEwan's use of symbolism becomes more explicit: for example, the Rolls Royce that drives Lola and Marshall away reappears in the next part; the wallpaper has 'pale vertical stripes, like a boy's pyjamas', which not only remind us of the pyjamas that Robbie thinks about in Part Two, but has clear connotations with

TASK

McEwan writes that 'nothing for certain was achieved'. To what extent do you agree with the following view: 'By Part 3 the narrative is so unreliable that readers no longer know what is "true" and what is "false".

Taking it further ▶

Robbie's arrival is described as a 'deliverance'; and Briony resolves to write a new 'draft', an 'atonement'. What do you think these words mean at this point in the novel?

prison bars, and the pale striped pyjamas worn by inmates in the Nazi death camps. The words that have until now seemed so intrinsic to Cecilia's love for Robbie ('Come back') are revealed to be the words that Cecilia said to Briony when she had a bad dream. It is a prosaic, even mundane, explanation of something that has previously been so potently romantic.

Part Three ends with Briony Tallis' initials, and a place and date: 'BT London 1999'. The preceding pages can now be seen for what they are: a fiction, written by Briony to atone for her crime. But how much of it is true, and how much is a lie (as far as such terms can be used in a novel), remains to be determined.

London, 1999

We are now in modern London, and Briony Tallis is 77 years old. She has just learned she has vascular dementia which means that she suffers a series of minor strokes. She says, 'my brain, my mind, is closing down'. Before this happens she has to complete 'those little tasks of housekeeping' that mark the 'reluctant process of letting go'. These involve going to the Imperial War Museum to return the resources she has used in writing her account of Robbie's and Cecilia's story.

Her visit to the Museum happens to coincide with one by the now elderly Paul and Lola (Lord and Lady) Marshall. He is frail, but she has 'a terrible agility' and Briony admits to herself that Lola will no doubt outlive her. This is important to her because it means that the true story of the rape cannot be published while Lola is still alive because it is libellous. Briony deliberately avoids making contact with them. After saying goodbye to staff she travels back to her flat in Regent's Park. Once there she reflects on her life and her late husband Thierry, and thinks about how, soon, she will not recognise his image. A car collects her from her flat to take her to a family gathering, arranged by Charles (Pierrot's grandson) in the old Tallis house, which is now a hotel.

She has been booked into Auntie Venus' room. From there she contemplates the changes made to the house and its grounds. She regrets some (such as the loss of the lake) but others are an improvement. She goes for drinks in the library (now stripped of its books) in the early evening, where she is met by 50 relatives. Leon is now in a wheelchair, partly paralysed by a stroke; Pierrot remains 'twinkly' (his brother, Jackson, died fifteen years before). Lola is not mentioned.

The various grandchildren have organised a surprise performance of *The Trials of Arabella*. Although it is 'not my best', Briony enjoys it. She gives a short speech of thanks before dinner, and then retires to her room where she reflects on the 'strange two days' which has seen her revisit her 'last novel

… that should have been my first'. We learn that Robbie was never rescued but died of septicaemia in Dunkirk, and that Cecilia was killed the same year when a bomb hit Balham Underground Station. Briony did not meet them at their flat: instead, she returned to the hospital after watching Lola's wedding to Marshall.

▲ We learn that a happy ending for Cecilia and Robbie has been engineered by Briony, and in fact Cecilia was killed at Balham Underground Station – probably while taking shelter from the Blitz

However, as she looks out of the window one last time, she thinks of Robbie being driven away by the police, and hopes that 'what really happened' is what she has written in her unpublished novel: that 'the lovers live', united at the end. That is her final act of kindness to them, her final act of atonement.

Commentary The title of this section connects us to Part Three, as well as to a specific time and place. Briony is now 77 years old and coming to the end of her writing career. Because of this she is forced to contemplate an author's responsibilities.

The sight of Lola and Marshall forces Briony to think again about her narrative, and for McEwan to redraw, yet again, the border between what he has written and what his character has invented. The conflict between appearance and reality is heightened throughout the novel, but even more so once we have read Connolly's letter. Lola, although 80 years old, is still in heels and in good health; this means that Briony's book cannot be published, thus ensuring that the 'truth' can never be known.

> **TASK**
> Briony writes that 'If I really cared so much about facts, I should have written a different kind of book'. What sort of book has 'she' written? Is it an autobiography? Is it a work of fiction? Or is it something else?

Briony: 'I count myself an unreliable narrator'

Briony's diagnosis of dementia partly explains some of the apparent lapses in the novel we have just read: for example, a colonel has pointed out to her that a 'Stuka does not carry a single thousand-ton bomb', but her error still stands in Part Two.

Familiar themes are again present: the conflict between appearance and reality, the passing of time, misinterpretation, justice – all can be seen as Briony attempts to come to terms with her past. In doing so, it allows McEwan to explore the limit of her account (it is hardly the 'forensic memoir' that she describes) and his own craft: is it the author's job to 'displace, transmute, dissemble'? Do the 'fogs of the imagination' conceal or reveal?

> What are novelists for? Go just so far as is necessary, set up camp inches beyond the reach, the fingertips of the law.

It is fitting that her first fiction – *The Trials of Arabella* – is finally preformed, as it forces Briony to reflect on her own development as a writer, and to answer the most fundamental question a narrator can ask: 'But what *really* happened?' It also provides a satisfying cyclical structure to the novel and establishes a sense of completion.

Build critical skills

To what extent do you think that McEwan's deliberate inclusion of errors in Briony's 'draft' adds greater authenticity to his own text? Or would you agree that it too obviously manipulates the reader?

Context

Cruella de Vil is, as her name suggests, the main villain in *The Hundred and One Dalmatians*, a novel by Dodie Smith published in 1956. It was made into a Disney animated film in 1961 and remains one of the most popular children's movies of all time.

TASK

Briony admits that she favours a 'pointillist approach to verisimilitude'. Research this genre of painting and think about how this might apply to the whole novel.

Briony's return to her old home gives her the opportunity to 'make a tidy finish', although such a statement could be meant ironically by McEwan, given the ambiguity of the text he has created. What really happened does not, for Briony, 'constitute an ending' in anything other than a novel 'of the bleakest realism'. She admits she no longer has 'the courage of [such] pessimism' and has, therefore, changed reality. In doing so she has been forced to think about the relationship the writer has with her subject matter, and has concluded that, very simply, a happy ending is better than a sad ending.

Taking it further ▶▶

McEwan asks: how can a novelist achieve atonement if 'she is God?' Read the paragraph on page 371 closely: what do you think he means? Think about 'the impossible task' he describes, and the conclusion that, ultimately, 'the attempt' is all that matters. How true is this of writing in general, and this novel in particular?

Briony has reunited Robbie and Cecilia in her writing, even though no such reunion happened, but she sees that as an act of kindness, not deception. Indeed if there is another draft of the novel then they could join the family celebrations in the library, 'still in love, sitting side by side'. The novelist has that power to transform and change and, within the parameters of the text they create, that is the only truth that matters.

In an interview McEwan says of atonement:

> *The word itself is fascinating. It's an eighteenth century made-up word meaning 'at onement' and I suppose it is religious originally: you are at one with God, you have made your peace with God, you have cleared your conscience, you're going to Heaven (or not). But it has acquired a secular sense as well, you have made peace with the world.*

CRITICAL VIEW

Read McEwan's comment on atonement. To what extent would you agree that atonement has been granted to Briony at the end of this novel? And by whom?

Target your thinking

- What themes and ideas does McEwan explore? (**AO1**)
- How does McEwan use narrative methods to develop themes? (**AO2**)
- How does McEwan use other methods to develop themes? (**AO2**)
- In what ways can you use your study of themes to engage with different opinions about the novel and its importance? (**AO5**)

Atonement

Unsurprisingly, atonement is a dominant theme in the novel. But it is important to understand that this act has a particular quality that goes beyond a simple form of forgiveness: when someone seeks atonement they wish to make amends to the person they have wronged. In this sense it can be a more tangible, more *constructed* and less abstract act than forgiveness. Atonement could be seen to serve the person who seeks it: it is a public act that others (including the victim) will witness, and this in turn might provoke a reciprocated act of forgiveness.

It is Briony who seeks atonement from Robbie and Cecilia, and her desire to obtain this shapes the plot development as well as the structure of the novel. We are told that her belief in Robbie's guilt lasted a few years ('A ruthless youthful forgetting, a wilful erasing, protected her well into her teens'); after this realisation, her decision not to go to Cambridge University but instead to become a nurse is her first act of atonement. Cecilia says as much in a letter to Robbie:

> I get the impression she's taken on nursing as a sort of penance …
> I think she wants to recant.

Briony can only understand forgiveness through growing up. But as a child, it is beyond her comprehension: indeed, she sees Cecilia 'forgive' Robbie, when in fact there is nothing for her to forgive. What Cecilia does is believe in his innocence, and that is quite different. It is another misreading in a novel that contains many. McEwan is asking us important questions, which we attempt to answer as we read the text *for the first time*. Of course, once we have finished this initial reading the questions are reframed, forcing us to ask them again in light of realising that the whole production of the novel is Briony's attempt to atone for her lie.

McEwan shows us how difficult it is to forgive someone: Robbie – a good man who rescues children and leads his men to safety – cannot forgive, and takes his hatred of Briony to the grave. Or at least Briony imagines that he does. And this added perspective – realised only when we read London 1999 – reveals something else, which is more troubling and even more difficult to resolve: how do we forgive ourselves? Briony is motivated out of an urge to rewrite the past, to change the ending so that it offers hope, and although she is able to do this it not only does not change her crime, it also exposes the limits of what she – and an author – can achieve.

In the final part, Briony writes:

> The problem these fifty-nine years has been this: how can a novelist achieve atonement when, with her absolute power of deciding outcomes, she is also God? There is no one, no entity or higher form that she can appeal to, to be reconciled with, or that can forgive her. There is nothing outside her.

Top ten quotation

McEwan is an atheist and a rationalist who cannot turn to God for forgiveness. For him:

> *Within one novel you can live inside many different people's heads, in a way that you of course cannot do in normal life. I think that quality of penetration into other consciousnesses lies at the heart of its moral quest. Knowing, or sensing what it's like to be someone else I think is at the foundations of morality … I really don't believe for a moment that our moral sense comes from a God … It's human, universal, [it's] being able to think our way into the minds of others.*

Briony's acts of atonement will help rewrite Robbie's own past: 'she would rewrite the past so that the guilty became the innocent'. In doing so he would be freed of guilt, free from the associated guilt that the war has brought.

She is not, however, the only character seeking atonement. Although the overriding emotion that Robbie has for the crime committed against him is hatred, in his final moments before he dies in Bray Dunes he considers how he might regain his lost innocence, and what acts might hasten this. The leg he sees caught in a tree takes on a greater significance now and he links it to his rescuing of the twins at the end of Part One. For Robbie this 'invisible baggage' of his past is real weight (the twin he carried home was 'so heavy!'), but also a figurative weight that he seeks to unload by helping others. In his feverish state he imagines gathering up the remains of the 'nice looking kid' killed by German bombers and put them to rest in peace. And this child becomes symbolic of all the lost children in the novel – including Robbie's younger self – who have been unjustly destroyed. Robbie seeks atonement not only for the crime against Lola he did not commit, but for the lives he could not save: he wishes for those he has seen die to turn to him and say:

> You tried to help us. You couldn't carry us across the field. You carried the twins, but not us, no. No, you are not guilty. No.

The tragedy for Robbie is that he never finds this forgiveness: he seeks atonement from those who cannot grant it, and he, like those he has just witnessed, dies before such amends can be made. But McEwan also introduces

Building critical skills

After reading the quotation (right), to what extent do you think that McEwan's novel is moral in its tone? What moral sense does it seek to explore? And at the end of the novel, are we – the reader – able to forgive the author for the postmodernist 'crime' he has committed against conventional, realist fiction?

here an idea that will be fully developed through Briony: namely, that we have within us the ability to imaginatively recreate the past. If we cannot attain atonement then we can try to reimagine what possibilities could exist if circumstances had been different. As Robbie lies dying, McEwan writes that:

> He forced his thoughts towards the new situation, the one that was supposed to make him happy.

It is not much, and is dependent on the actions of others (and most obviously the author), but it is better than total despair.

Robbie's last thoughts, although dreamlike, revisit and develop important themes. They also, inevitably, contain many references to Cecilia. She, too, has sought a form of atonement through becoming a nurse and rejecting her family. When she writes that for Briony 'to go into nursing, to cut herself off from her background' is an act of recantation she is also describing her own actions. She has turned against her parents because they turned against him: 'there had to be a choice – you or them': and because they could not forgive him, she cannot forgive them.

Paul Marshall's crime is the most serious of all. We assume (because Briony tells us) that he did rape Lola, although the extent to which it is consensual is never established. Either way, it is clear that he has attacked her several times, and that he has sex with an underage girl. He is, along with Robbie, the only other character who knows for certain that Robbie is entirely innocent (Lola seems uncertain about who attacked her and is persuaded by Briony that it was Robbie), but he still allows him to go to jail. His act of atonement is commented on by Briony in the final pages when she sees (the now) Lord and Lady Marshall leaving the Imperial War Museum:

> It has often been remarked upon, how much good he did in the world. Perhaps he's spent a lifetime making amends.

These final pages – in which we see again the now elderly but still married Marshalls – raises some difficult questions for the reader. Is McEwan conceding that rape is excusable as long as the attacker undergoes some process of atonement (in Marshall's case, marriage to the victim and various acts of charity)? Additionally, is Briony's cold tone towards them to be trusted? After all, although she alone knows the nature of his crime she is unable to publish anything about it because of libel laws. The law has silenced her, at least until they die. Where, McEwan seems to be asking, is the justice here? Furthermore, if Briony was able to publish, what would be her real motive? To expose a crime? Or to clear her own conscience? Would it be an act of revenge, or an act of goodness?

We sense that these acts of goodness fail in their ultimate aim of gaining forgiveness from those who were sinned against: perhaps only a higher force – in this case, the author – can make the guilty atone for their crimes. However, we can see from the final section that it is not as straightforward as this.

Justice

Closely linked to atonement is justice. For Briony, 'the principles of justice' were important elements of *The Trials of Arabella*, and this 'love of order' partly explains why she wants to ensure that we are aware of the crimes committed, and that at each point the justice system fails, unable to cope with the seriousness of the crime committed. The initial process of questioning ('the interrogation') that follows the disappearance of the twins is flawed from the start: Marshall's ability to use his status and wealth to influence the police is subtly described; Emily Tallis 'belonged to a generation that treated policemen as menials'. This is a process that is riven with prejudices and preconceptions: the (mostly male) gathering ('an adult cabal') judges and condemns Cecilia and Robbie before a court can. By the time that Robbie returns with the twins, his fate seems decided. Even before he gets into the police car, handcuffed, Briony compares the process to 'eternal damnation'. McEwan seems to be suggesting that the law works well for the wealthy and the male, but it fails if you are, like Cecilia, female or, like Robbie, lower class.

McEwan is fascinated by the law (one of his later novels, *The Children Act*, has as its central character a female judge). It is worth considering what role the law, and those that enforce it, have in the novel. Many are absent, including the judge, barrister and jury who find Robbie guilty, and also the prison guards who limit his freedom. Then there is the extended apparatus of the state, including senior civil servants (such as Jack Tallis), the politicians who take the country to war, and the 'top brass' responsible for Dunkirk. Each of these upholds the laws of the land, and each create another narrative outside the acts of morality acted out by the main characters, but these narratives have their own momentum and are equally flawed.

Wherever we encounter man-made justice in the novel (including its symbols, such as the police, or, later, the military police) it is inadequate: it does not matter whether the policeman in the local village is a comic figure with a waxed moustache, or a senior inspector with 'a watchful unmoving mask' for a face. The innocent are condemned and the guilty remain free.

The parallels between the law and literature are evident throughout the novel. For McEwan the legal system, with its dramas, characters and grand themes of justice, revenge, life and death, remind him of writing. In an interview he remembers reading a book of legal judgments:

> *It was the prose that struck me first. Clean, precise, delicious. Serious, of course, compassionate at points, but lurking within its intelligence was something like humour, or wit, derived perhaps from its godly distance, which in turn reminded me of a novelist's omniscience.*

Natural – or divine – justice is equally flawed. God is almost entirely absent from *Atonement*, and when his name is invoked it is usually as a mild oath ('Oh my God!' or 'For God's sake'), or to give a rather empty endorsement of the

▲ Who receives justice in *Atonement*?

Taking it further ▶

Think about McEwan's
statement on page 34:
after reading the novel,
who do you think is
most responsible for
administering justice?
The legal system?
Briony? McEwan?
Or someone (and
something) else? What
tensions can be found
between these different
forms of justice within
the novel?

wedding between Marshall and Lola ('Send thy blessing upon thy servants, this man and woman'). The 'heavenly powers' addressed by the vicar in his 'weary' voice, the 'Author of everlasting life', is missing from the retreat from Dunkirk where random acts of violence result in so many innocent deaths. The ultimate source of power in this novel is not God but the author: Briony is 'a god' to the animals she sees on the evening of the rape, but even she is 'loitering on the periphery of their world', disengaged. There is 'no one, no entity or higher form that she can appeal to, or be reconciled with, or that can forgive her. There is nothing outside her', no God other than herself. Such a realisation invests the author with responsibility, but it is both liberating and isolating.

Misinterpretation

Atonement is a novel about writing and reading. Briony's ambitions to become a writer eventually come true, but in that process she (and we) understand how dangerous and unstable words are and, importantly, how easy it is to misinterpret them. For the young Briony words resemble something miraculous:

> A story was a form of telepathy. By means of inking symbols onto a page, she was able to send thoughts and feelings from her mind to her reader's. It was a magical process, so commonplace that no one stopped to wonder at it. Reading a sentence and understanding it were the same thing.

But they are *not* the same thing, and the gap between reading something and fully understanding its meaning is sometimes too great for not only Briony, but for other characters as well.

Cecilia misinterprets Robbie's intentions when he entered the Tallis house one day and took off his shoes and socks: for her it was a clumsy way of drawing attention to their different social class. For Robbie it was an entirely innocent act. Cecilia's recollection of this incident occurs at the fountain, and contributes to her desire to exact some revenge. It is this pivotal moment which is the most misread of all: within the text it has three observers (Robbie, Cecilia and Briony), but it has an unspecified number of other readers (Cyril Connolly, Elizabeth Bowen, the elder Briony, and us). That it is misread by each 'reader' emphasises how central this theme is to understanding the novel.

Robbie thinks that Cecilia's decision to strip off to her underwear in front of him to retrieve the broken parts of the vase was done 'to humiliate him'. For Cecilia her actions are to punish him, to deny him seeking amends (or atonement). Briony also observes what happens and fails to understand what it is she has seen ('the sequence was illogical') and she senses, on reflection, that 'she could write a scene like the one by the fountain', which of course she does (and which in turn is rejected by Cyril Connolly in Part Three when we learn that the described scene has been written and rewritten by the older Briony).

Taking it further ▶▶

Briony considers writing the fountain scene 'three times over, from three points of view'. This three-sided perspective adds to the triangular motif that reoccurs in the novel: Pierrot is missing a triangle of flesh from his left ear; the vase splits into two 'triangular' pieces; Cecilia smooths a 'jagged triangle of paper' and thinks about 'how her little sister was changing'; and Robbie glimpses 'the triangular darkness' of her pubic hair. Comment on McEwan's use of such symbolism.

The story that Briony eventually rewrites as *Two Figures by a Fountain* forces us to re-evaluate the reality of what happened: it is a redrafted version of experience, changed on the advice of an editor to make it more believable. But is it true? Briony is usually involved in each episode of misinterpretation. It is she who misreads the letter that Robbie mistakenly sends to her sister (as indeed do Emily, Leon and the police); whereas Cecilia sees it as something erotic, for Briony it is 'disgusting'. She also misreads her sister's expression of ecstasy as of terror in the library. But it is her interpretation of the assaults on Lola that proves to be her most damaging misreading of all. Briony makes the mistake of believing that it is enough to know, without having the ocular proof to support it: she is surprised by the 'austere view of the visual' that the police have, preferring instead something more intuitive ('less like seeing, more like knowing').

Marshall's first assault results in bruising up to Lola's elbows, but Briony sees them as something less troubling ('Chinese burns'). She then interprets (and reinterprets) the rape so that it fits her own narrative; however, it is a story constructed in darkness ('it was not possible to read expressions') and inevitably only partially understood.

Appropriately, it is Robbie, with his First in English Literature, who seems the most accurate reader. It is he who notices the 'two-inch scratch' on Marshall's face; he who has written poetry and does not limit himself to any single interpretation of life but, instead, ranges across medicine, psychology, literature and philosophy; he who, crucially, is able to navigate territory using only a 'compass with slitted sighting mirror'; he who can 'study' a map, with 'no doubts', and lead his men to safety.

Ultimately, though, it is us – the readers – who find ourselves guilty of a misreading which challenges us to re-evaluate the whole novel. When we realise that Briony has revised her novella on the advice of Cyril Connolly, it exposes the artifice behind the text: we have 'misread' the narrative, initially believing it to be a story about Robbie's and Cecilia's (eventual) reunion. The 'truth' is, of course, that they both die apart. It is Briony Tallis, a self-confessed 'unreliable witness', who is the author of these deceptions and, as she says in the novel's final lines, further interpretations remain possible if the 'route map' her doctor has given her allows her to.

Atonement is a novel not just about a writer (Briony), but also about writing. There are many writers referred to, and their writing style at times directly

TASK

How many other episodes are there in the novel when appearance and reality do not cohere? How many different forms of reading – and misreading – can you think of? Consider what this says about the importance McEwan places on evidence.

TASK

How many other instances of misinterpretation can you find in the novel? What are the results of these mistakes?

Taking it further ▶

What do you think
McEwan means by this,
and how much would
you agree with his last
statements? Some
have criticised him for
subverting the 'given
terms of the illusion of
fiction'. To what extent
do McEwan's views help
you to understand his
methodology in this novel?

influences Briony's (and McEwan's) own style (Virginia Woolf being the most
obvious example). Why does McEwan do this? To write a novel about writing a
novel risks being too inward-looking, and he recognises this:

> *I think I'm always drawn to some kind of balance between a fiction
> that is self-reflective on its own processes, and one that has a forward
> impetus too, that will completely accept the given terms of the illusion
> of fiction. I've never been interested in that kind of fiction that
> triumphantly declares that art is not life. Only novelists ever think that
> art is life. Readers never have any problems with it.*

Sex is often badly misunderstood by the novel's main characters. Before reading
Robbie's letter, Briony finds sexual bliss 'unthinkable'; Robbie's sighting of a
near-naked Cecilia results in him 'fetishising the love object', referring to Freud,
Keats, Shakespeare and Petrarch as a way of understanding the 'symptoms'
of sexual attraction. The justice system that had resulted in his conviction
compounds the error by diagnosing him 'with clinical precision' as 'morbidly
over-sexed'. As a result he and Cecilia have to revert to writing in code to
disguise the 'sexual ecstasy' they dream of experiencing once again. In addition,
the sexual acts that occur in this novel are ambiguously described: we do not
know if Lola is raped, and Cecilia's and Robbie's sexual encounter in the library
is both interrupted and, to Briony, appears to be an act of violence. But what
they have in common is that both are open to misinterpretation.

Innocence and experience

Growing up – moving from a state of innocence to one of experience –
dominates *Atonement*. Both Briony and Lola believe that they are adults, when
in fact Briony is still a child and Lola is an adolescent. These mistakenly held
self-perceptions cause many of the problems in the book. The mistakes Briony
makes are a result of her being a 'busy, priggish, conceited little girl' who cannot
accept the limitations of her understanding. We are made aware of her failings
by the elder Briony – the mature author who rewrites and reinterprets the
actions on that fateful day in 1935 when she was only thirteen.

It is Briony's 'innocent intensity' which makes her 'particularly vulnerable to
failure'; she is unable to retain any perspective on events, preferring instead
to adapt what she sees to her own limited understanding of human behaviour.
In her writings, innocence is an end in itself because it retains the status
quo: her 'heroines and heroes reached their innocent climaxes and needed
to go no further'. Such a view is unrealistic of course, and innocence can be
damaging: the twins threaten to 'wreck the play innocently', Danny Hardman's
lips are 'innocently cruel'. This unpredictability is typical of adolescent
behaviour, and, ironically, it is Robbie who recognises this before it wrecks his
life. He observes:

> At this stage in her life Briony inhabited an ill-defined transitional space between the nursery and adult worlds which she crossed and recrossed unpredictably.

Top Ten quotation

For the older Briony, part of the act of atonement is to 'rewrite the past so that the guilty became the innocent'. In this way she is able to restore the sense of order that she has always desired. Experience, or adulthood, is associated with certainty, and it is this desire that motivates her to behave as she does: she is conscious, as she holds Robbie's letter in her hands, that she is 'entering an arena of adult emotion'. No sooner has she read it than we witness a sudden fall from innocence: the knowledge that the 'shock' of the words convey results in her feeling 'guilt'. Within a paragraph she has moved from thinking about fairy tales to contemplating a world where there 'are no more princesses': instead, 'something elemental, brutal, perhaps even criminal had been introduced'.

Build critical skills

After Lola has lied to Briony that the twins have attacked her (when in fact it was Marshall trying to abuse her) Briony thinks about advising on changing out of a dress 'that made it so difficult to walk'. She decides against it, concluding that 'attaining adulthood was all about the eager acceptance of such impediments'. What do you think McEwan means by this?

Lola is even more convinced that she is grown up than Briony. But even so, she has to adopt the 'guise of the adult she considered herself at heart to be'. Her clothes are sophisticated and other 'tokens of maturity' are intended to convey the impression that her 'nearly adult mind' deserves to be treated more seriously than a child's. McEwan describes her presence as 'potent', and this barely disguised sexuality is, like Briony's misplaced understanding of the world, at times difficult to predict and control.

It is of course sex that is central to distinguishing the innocent child from the experienced adult (only the twins seem entirely free of such thoughts, even doing 'clownish eye-rolling yawns' at Lola's marriage to Marshall). But sex is an unstable, even dangerous, impulse that can barely be controlled: Marshall assaults Lola because he cannot control himself; but Lola, too, seems unable to control her emerging sexuality. Robbie's encounter with Cecilia in the library is another example of uncontrollable emotions, and each of these events has disastrous consequences. Other relationships between men and women seem broken (the Quinceys are going through an acrimonious divorce) or passionless (Jack and Emily Tallis have a sexless marriage). McEwan seems to be suggesting that when it comes to sex, no character in the novel behaves in a mature or responsible way.

Build critical skills

Even the twins understand that when adulthood and childhood are blurred: for them Marshall 'had no business with sweets'. Explore the different relationships between adults and children in this novel and think about which are healthy, and which are not. What do you think McEwan is saying about growing up?

Conflict

For McEwan's fictionalised version of Cyril Connolly, 'warfare … is the enemy of creative activity'. Such sentiments should be viewed ironically because *Atonement* is a subtle analysis of many different forms of conflict. The novel begins in 1935, a time when tensions in Europe were already rising because of the growing threat from Nazi Germany. Outwardly, the Tallis home is a peaceful one, but into it arrive the Quincey children, 'refugees from a bitter domestic civil war'. The divorce their parents are undergoing is not the only domestic dispute: Emily and Jack Tallis ('the household protector') have a distant relationship which resembles a cold war; Marshall attacks Lola several times, and even Briony acts violently as she thrashes away at nettles, dreaming of 'sacrificing' the twins and Lola. Violence seems to be an innate part of human identity: it is as present in bucolic Surrey as it is in war-torn northern France.

McEwan is also interested in the consequences of these conflicts, and how characters respond to them, as the acts of aggression themselves. It is significant that both Briony and Cecilia are nurses: to some extent they are both seeking atonement, but we are clearly meant to admire this commitment to helping others. In its strict enforcement of rules, its loss of identity where only surnames are used and uniforms replace civilian clothes, the profession was a female version of the (then) entirely masculine armed forces. But there is a crucial difference: whereas soldiers kill, nurses save.

Such engagement is certainly more admirable than the response that Cyril Connolly suggests writers should adopt, when he tells Briony that it is 'wise and right to ignore [war] and devote themselves to other subjects'.

The novel itself is a lengthy description of the *reaction* to conflict: the argument over a broken vase, the assault on Lola, the bombing of Dunkirk. Like his main protagonist, McEwan traces the 'lines of branching consequences to the point before the destruction' begins, to their original motives.

TASK

War is described in unforgiving detail in Parts Two and Three of *Atonement*, and many of the characters are involved in turbulent relationships. However, Jack and Emily Tallis have a sterile marriage that endures because of a 'dread of conflict'. To what extent do you think McEwan's description of human relationships is entirely without hope?

Characters

Target your thinking

- How does McEwan develop his characters as the narrative progresses? (**AO1**)
- In what ways does McEwan use narrative methods to shape the reader's responses to his characters? (**AO2**)
- How do you and other readers respond to the ways in which McEwan presents characters? (**AO5**)

Briony Tallis

Briony Tallis is not only the novel's protagonist, she is also its 'author'. As such, she is responsible for the pivotal moments in the plot: delivering Robbie's letter to Cecilia, discovering Robbie and Cecilia making love and, most importantly, falsely accusing Robbie of raping Lola Quincey. The first two contribute to her mistaken belief that she is 'entering an arena of adult emotion' and can make mature judgements.

Briony is the only character we meet as a child, as a young adult and as an old woman. At thirteen she is the youngest child of Emily and Jack, and sister to Cecilia and Leon. The elderly Briony of the final section describes her teenage self as a 'busy, priggish, conceited little girl', but she is also a romantic (who has a crush on Robbie when she is ten), and has a passion for secrets. She is 'one of those children possessed by a desire to have the world just so'. This results in her trying to impose meaning on 'an untidy world', which results in disaster for Robbie.

After reading Robbie's letter she thinks that he is 'disgusting', making it easier for her to accuse him of being a rapist. Briony tells Lola of Robbie's letter, but crucially misreads the signs of assault her cousin has received from Marshall. It is Briony who convinces Lola that it is Robbie who raped her, and although Briony later seeks forgiveness for her actions we are left in no doubt that she enjoyed the 'vile excitement' of being at the centre of the adults' attention. She had the opportunities to change her evidence, but chooses not to.

Such misreadings and poor decisions are of course essential to the plot. But how much of a 'villain' is Briony? Yes, she enjoys the sense of power that being a key witness brings, but it is Briony who is hardest on herself, and the most unforgiving: it is she, more than any other character, who seeks atonement. How we judge her crime, and her sense of guilt, to a great extent defines our understanding of the novel itself.

Taking it further ▶

McEwan has said that 'Style is an extension of personality'. To what extent do you think that the language used by Briony is an accurate extension of her personality? Give evidence from the text to support your argument.

▲ Juno Temple as Lola and Saoirse Ronan as Briony in the 2007 film *Atonement*

Her actions in Part One explain why she decides to become a nurse at St Thomas' Hospital rather than study at Cambridge University. It is an act of atonement. But she still has aspirations to be a writer and sends her story – *Two Figures by a Fountain* – to *Horizon* magazine. It is when she receives Cyril Connolly's rejection letter that we learn that she has written Part One of the novel to change the fates of those whose lives she has ruined.

In her fictionalised account, she meets Robbie and Cecilia in wartime London and promises them to withdraw her evidence. But the meeting does not take place and both die without being reunited.

Briony becomes a successful writer. In the final section, set in London in 1999 and in the old Tallis home, she admits that she has a form of dementia. This novel is her act of atonement to Robbie and Cecilia.

Cecilia Tallis

Cecilia is 23 years old, and is the Tallises' middle child. At the beginning of the novel she is newly returned from Girton College, Cambridge, where she has been studying English Literature. Her summer has been spent 'wasting her days'. Breaking Uncle Clem's vase is a crucial moment because it sets in motion a series of events that result in her and Robbie – who she has known since childhood – falling in love. Her response to this accident is also telling: she does not hesitate from stripping off her clothes and diving in to retrieve the submerged fragments. She is decisive and self-confident. She is also attractive: Robbie lingers over her semi-naked form in great detail, seeing even her blemishes as 'adornments', and although as a young woman her long face could be described as 'horsey', she grows into being 'boldly sensual'. She takes great care over her appearance, but in her 'fierce' returning of young Hardman's staring shows that she does so on her terms, rather than for the benefit of men.

Build critical skills

McEwan's representation of girls and women in *Atonement* is worth exploring because each is clearly defined and has very different characteristics which we could loosely define as feminine. What adjectives and adverbs immediately come to mind when you think about the main female characters? To what extent are these descriptions favourable or unfavourable?

Cecilia becomes ▶ increasingly distant from her family as the novel continues

Cecilia's temper flairs up on a number of occasions: she is initially irritated by her father funding Robbie to go through medical school (which partly explains the tension between the two), but she loses her temper with Briony at supper (calling her 'a tiresome prima donna'), and also with the police and her family when she realises they have all read Robbie's letter (she looks at them with 'red-eyed contempt'). But she is willing to help others, and is loyal. It is she who often comforts her younger sister when she has bad dreams, and also offers to help the twins when they have been neglected by their parents, and Lola. She also believes in Robbie's innocence, writing regularly to him when he is prison, and in France, finishing each letter with the same words: 'I'll wait for you. Come back.'

It is because of this loyalty to Robbie that Cecilia cuts herself off from her family, and although Robbie is uncomfortable with this decision she does not waver, explaining that 'when they wrecked your life they wrecked mine'. Her loyalty to him is unfaltering. In a novel where justice is so important, Cecilia seems to offer something close to the blind, unbiased objectivity to the crime that others lack (her name is derived from the Latin *caecus*, meaning 'blind'). Strong, independent but ultimately doomed, Cecilia has a degree of integrity that others lack. Her loyalty to Robbie, although admirable, brings her nothing but pain. For McEwan this could be another sign of the randomness to existence, where there is no justice beyond man's own flawed form. But hope does exist for Cecilia, if only Briony, before she does shut down, lets her 'lovers live' and 'unite[s] them at the end'.

Robbie Turner

Robbie is the son of Grace and Ernest Turner. He is 24 years old at the start of the novel. His father walked out on his wife and young son soon after the birth, never to be seen again. Since then Jack Tallis has felt a sense of duty to the Turners, keeping Grace on as a servant and funding Robbie to study English at Cambridge and then medicine. Robbie has 'a first-rate mind', gaining the best degree in his year. Briony describes him as 'startlingly handsome', with 'sunken' cheeks 'like an Indian brave's'. We first see him as he is establishing his own identity in the world: he has abandoned many 'fads' (even joining the Communist Party at one stage) but when he sets out for the fateful meal at the Tallis home he is optimistic about his career as a doctor. For McEwan he is the personification of the lives unlived, the millions who have their hopes crushed by an indifferent universe: personal tragedies (such as Briony's accusation) can combine with universal tragedies (such as war), often making a mockery of the hopes we all hold. Only a writer can give life to the rich interior worlds inhabited, briefly, by those who never lived to see them fulfilled.

Whatever hope he has lasts a matter of hours. As soon as he gives the wrong letter to Briony, his fate takes another course. He is compared by McEwan to 'a faithful moth, trying to choose the less disastrous of two poor options', but it says something about his bravery that he decides to attend the meal. It is, however, the first of many wrong decisions he takes that evening. Cecilia's response is unexpected: she is not insulted; instead she draws him to her, and they make love in the library. They are interrupted by Briony, which results in him hating her for the first (but not last) time. This burning, lasting hatred of Briony adds to the complexity of his characterisation: he is no angel, no innocent capable of forgiveness. Such emotions make him more real to us.

At the meal Robbie is consumed with thoughts of what has just happened, but it does not stop him being the first to notice the long scratch on Marshall's face, nor to ask why he had not reported Lola's injuries earlier. He is perceptive but, unfortunately, is not listened to enough. His next mistake is to search for the missing twins alone, and although he finds and returns them, this decision 'transformed his life', leading him to be accused of rape for which he had no alibi.

He is sent to jail and serves three-and-a-half years of his sentence, before 'bargaining an early release in return for joining the infantry'. He survives this ordeal, emerging as a damaged but still commanding figure. Even after he is separated from his regiment (the West Kents) in France he imposes his natural authority on Nettle and Mace (who are higher in rank than Robbie) to lead them to Dunkirk and possible rescue. His journey ends in a cellar where he dies of septicaemia, dreaming of being reunited with Cecilia, and although his name is never publicly cleared we learn from these pages of his innocence, and his enduring love.

Leon Tallis

Leon Tallis is 25 years old and the oldest of the Tallis children; of the three he seems the most innocent. His mother regards him as 'too handsome, too popular'; for him 'no one is mean-spirited, no one schemed or lied or betrayed'. Unlike his sisters – and Robbie – he is not an intellectual: 'literature and politics, science and religion, did not bore him – they simply had no place in his world'. Kind though he is to his mother, he believes that his prospects are 'diminishing by the year': he refused the 'offer of a leg-up from his father, the chance of something decent in the civil service, preferring instead to be the humblest soul in a private bank'. He enjoys rowing and likes telling anecdotes. Leon's life is 'a polished artefact'. It is perhaps ironic that his name derives from 'lion': rather than being brave and fierce Leon seems passive, even timid.

Unknowingly, Leon changes the direction of everyone's lives by bringing Paul Marshall to the Tallis home and inviting Robbie to the evening dinner. This lack of foresight changes on the night of the attack. It is Leon who picks up Lola after the attack and it is he to whom Briony begins to tell her story. During the questioning by the police, Leon (in the eyes of Briony herself) asserts himself, conferring with the doctor to 'murmur a manly summary of event'. Briony watches and wonders, 'where was Leon's carefree lightness now?' He also takes charge, instructing his father over the telephone to return from London, and preparing his mother for the shocking news. But all of these actions are redrafted versions by Briony of what might have happened: each small action, every tiny event which is outside her control, to some extent lifts her guilt a little more. The patterns of behaviour we observe in Part One have been drawn by a narrator desperate to accept blame and also shift some of it to others, including her family.

Leon fades from the narrative from this point. We learn that he had tried to make contact with Cecilia once, 'but she would not speak to him'. Perhaps his lion-like qualities did surface, but only in the domestic (rather than military) arena: in the final section Briony tells us that he 'heroically nursed his wife', raising his boisterous children alone. He married four times, but by the end of the novel, having suffered from a stroke, he is barely able to do much more than smile.

Emily Tallis

Emily Tallis is 46 years old and is the mother to Leon, Cecilia and Briony. She suffers from debilitating migraines – 'knifing pains' that can 'obliterate all thought' – and because of these she often retreats to her darkened bedroom. There, she tends to worry about herself, her family, her marriage. Resigned to growing 'stiffer in the limbs and more irrelevant by the day', she is caught in a loveless marriage: her husband is usually absent, sometimes forgetting even to call her during the day. Such issues tend not to lower her spirits; instead she seems to float above them, 'absently braiding them with other preoccupations'.

Emily has mostly led a sheltered life: 'educated at home until the age of sixteen' before being sent to a school in Switzerland for one year; she remains sceptical of women going to university. When she is well enough, she does her best to support her children, especially Briony ('to love her was to be soothed'). Emily is less forgiving of her elder daughter, whom she thinks is wasting her time (and remains without a husband), and Leon (who has 'no sting of unhappiness and ambition'). Most of her scorn, however, is reserved for her younger sister Hermione: she thinks of her as a 'stealer of scenes, little mistress of histrionics'. In contrast, Emily is the 'scowling, silent, older sister', the 'wronged child, wronged wife'.

Build critical skills

To what extent are we supposed to sympathise with Emily? Compared to the pain and trauma that her daughters undergo, her pain seems self-indulgent. But is McEwan asking us to look beyond this first impression? Should we look at her physical and emotional isolation from her family as something tragic? Is her sad, lonely life a result of her position in society at the time: an upper-middle class wife of a senior civil servant, unable to work and incapable of changing her life?

Like Leon, she 'untypically' rises to the challenges that arrive on the night of Lola's assault: 'she actually grew as her older daughter shrank into private misery'. But also like Leon this evening is effectively the last time we see her. We know from Briony that she continued to write to her during the war, but we also learn that she died before Jack, in 1974, and she is recalled only through some mementos owned by Briony (such as a 'cameo brooch').

Lola Quincey

Lola Quincey is the sister of Jackson and Pierrot Quincey, and the cousin to the three Briony children. At the beginning of the novel she is fifteen years old and 'a refugee from a bitter domestic civil war'. She is described as having ginger hair, 'green eyes and sharp bones in her face, and hollow cheeks' but like Cecilia she also has 'a temper easily lost'. She dresses like an adult, wearing perfume and an ankle bracelet, and is 'perfectly composed'. During the rehearsals for the play, Lola cleverly manipulates events so that she becomes Arabella, the central character. Briony is powerless to stop it ('the advance of Lola's dominion was merciless'). She is clearly Marshall's victim, but she also flirts with him in Chapter 5, misreading how dangerous he is (tellingly, she associates the Amo bar with love, rather than recognising it as an abbreviation of ammunition).

She does nothing to clear Robbie's name. Indeed, Marshall has attacked her before, but when in Chapter 10 she tries to convey to Briony what has happened, she fails to do so. It seems like a rehearsal for the real attack: again, it involves Briony, and again Lola allows her cousin to influence her, 'meekly' accepting that it was Robbie who raped her. Perhaps she has a reason for reacting in this way.

Lola, more than any other character, exists on the fault line between adulthood and childhood: it is a dangerous place, for her and for others who misinterpret her intentions. She and her brothers seem alien to the Tallis household (even her name, derived from the Spanish, is exotic). For McEwan, who from the very beginning of his career has explored the tensions between innocence and experience (see, for example, one of his most famous novels, *The Child in Time*), Lola's actions forces us to ask difficult questions about sexuality and guilt: for example, to what extent is she partly responsible not only for the assault (does she encourage Marshall?), but also Robbie's conviction (could she really not know it was not him?)

Only in Part Three do we discover that Lola and Marshall are to marry, which further suggests she was not entirely innocent on that fateful night in Part One. She has, for Briony, 'saved herself from humiliation by falling in love', allowing her to 'marry her rapist'. They stay married for the rest of their lives, and our last view of her is as Lady Marshall disappearing with her husband into a Rolls Royce. Now nearly 80 she is 'still as lean and fit as a racing dog'. Heavily made up, she has become cartoon-like, reminiscent of Cruella de Vil. There is no reconciliation with her family, and her continued good health ensures that Briony's story of Robbie and Cecilia can never be published in case it libels her and her husband.

▲ The sexual connection between Lola and Paul Marshall is ambiguous and troubling, given Lola's age

Paul Marshall

Paul Marshall's first appearance establishes his ambiguousness: his face is 'comically brooding' (it is later described as 'cruel'), his conversation 'conventionally dull'. He is self-important, talking in a 'ten-minute monologue' about how successful and rich he is becoming as a chocolate-bar manufacturer. He is 'almost handsome', but also 'unfathomably stupid'. The drinks he makes for Robbie and Cecilia are 'viscous brown' and disgusting. He could be a comical figure, but there is something more unsettling to him: Cecilia is conscious of his stare when they first meet, and Chapter 4 ends with him possibly touching her arm.

This sense of sexual threat develops. He has an erotic dream about his sisters shortly before taking a libidinous interest in Lola, seeing her as 'almost a young woman … quite the little Pre-Raphaelite princess'. He attacks Lola once before (possibly) raping her, and it is clear that each attack is violent (after the first, Lola is 'bruised up to [her] elbows'). After he assaults her outside, he ingratiates himself with the police, impressing them with money and offering cigarettes from his 'gold case'.

> ### TASK
> The night of the assault is described by Briony, but we have seen that throughout the novel different perspectives offer different stories. How else could the relationship between Marshall and Lola be viewed? Has Briony written a revisionist interpretation of events in order to make her actions more understandable? Or, to put it another way, if there was no rape, and the act was consensual, how would this alter your view of Briony's crime and Robbie's fate?

We see him for the last time, aged 88, with his wife outside the Imperial War Museum. Still 'cruelly handsome' he is 'reduced' by age, 'a little doddery', using a stick to walk. He has given much of his money away causing Briony to wonder if he has done so 'to make amends' – another form of atonement.

Jack Tallis

Jack Tallis is the most important character who never appears in the novel. He remains in Whitehall throughout the novel, helping prepare the country for war. Like the senior civil servant he is, his influence can be felt at a distance: it is he who sponsors Robbie to study at Cambridge, and it is he who gives Grace Turner her bungalow. Although physically absent he accurately assesses the seriousness of the missing twins, deciding to call the police as Emily dithers. Tellingly, though, he never makes it back to the house: his car breaks down en route. He marries again after Emily dies but there seems to be little lasting affection for him from Briony: she tries to telephone him to talk to him about Lola's marriage to Marshall, but they are, in every sense, unable to 'connect'.

Jackson Quincey and Pierrot Quincey

The twins are nine years old when they arrive at the Tallis household. They are almost identical, both in appearance (apart from Pierrot missing a triangle of skin from his ear) and behaviour. Like their sister they are ginger and freckled, and cause Briony much distress when rehearsing the play (Pierrot claiming that acting is 'just showing off'). Also like their sister they seem rather alien: their names are different, less Anglo-Saxon than some of the other characters (Pierrot is a character from French pantomime and *commedia dell'arte*, traditionally having a white face and sad expression).

They are emotionally damaged by their parents' divorce (Jackson wets the bed 'as troubled small boys far from home will'), and we are able to understand why they run away when we realise how neglected they are: Cecilia sees how 'hopeless and terrifying it was for them to be without love'. But it is their decision to run away that adds a new energy to Part One of the novel, creating chaos which is only momentarily resolved by Robbie finding them. The twins make a swift reappearance at the wedding of Lola and Marshall: they are 'delighted to see her', and their other actions confirm that they are the only children in the novel who behave innocently. We see Pierrot one last time in the party that his grandson, Charles, has organised for Briony: he is 'much shrivelled' but full of life. Jackson had died fifteen years earlier. Minor characters though they are, both seem to exemplify still further McEwan's belief that actions have unintended consequences.

Grace Turner

Grace Turner is Robbie's mother. She became the Tallises' cleaner 'the week after Ernest [her husband] walked away'. She raised Robbie alone, supplementing her income with some clairvoyance work for 'women who came for a shilling's glimpse of the future' (her name, which has so many connotations, is clearly linked to some form of spirituality). Although the Tallis family laugh at her 'dedication to the surface of things', it is Grace who sees the truth of the false claims made about her son: she 'roars' that they are all 'Liars! Liars! Liars!' at the end of Part One. She remains loyal to her son, and is the only guest he is allowed to have during the three-and-a-half years he is in jail.

Danny Hardman

Danny Hardman is a young 'handyman', and the son of a long-established family servant. There is a sexual threat to him: Briony and Lola are both aware of his eyes lingering on them. Both Robbie and Cecilia think that it is he, not Marshall, who raped Lola. When they discover the truth, Robbie admits that they owe 'Able Seaman Hardman' an apology. But, like Robbie himself, it is too late as he has been killed in action, serving in the Royal Navy.

Betty

Betty is the Tallis family's cook. Although 'distant and firm' she has 'a kindly heart' but one 'which no child would ever discover'. She complains loudly about having to make a roast dinner at the height of summer, and it is this meal which acts as an ominous prelude to the events of the fateful evening. In a letter to Briony, Emily describes how Betty accidentally dropped Uncle Clem's vase, smashing it to pieces.

Corporal Nettle and Corporal Mace

These two men accompany Robbie on his last journey through France. Although they outrank him, they follow him, seeing him as a 'toff'. Although both are hardened soldiers, they are essentially kind (both dig a grave for a young boy they have seen killed in Dunkirk) and protective (Mace rescues the stricken RAF pilot moments before he would have been killed by an angry mob). It is Nettle who stays with Robbie right to the end, and it is also 'Mr Nettle' who writes a number of long letters to Briony, giving her details of the final moments of Robbie's life and the retreat of the British forces at Dunkirk.

Writer's methods: form, structure and language

Target your thinking

- Consider the methods that McEwan uses and how are they used to shape meaning and to create effects? (**AO2**)
- How can you use literary terminology to help you to articulate your responses with more precision and concision? (**AO1**)
- In what ways can different close readings that engage with McEwan's methods lead to alternative interpretations? (**AO5**)

Structure

The four parts of *Atonement* act like semi-autonomous novellas: they have their own intricate plot lines and main characters, but each overlap and inform the other. The links between each part are not immediately apparent, and it is only after reading several pages of each that we find out where we are, and how the narrative has progressed. The final part is, stylistically, very different from the previous three parts (for a start, it is written in the first person) and changes how we view the whole novel.

Taking it further ▶▶

As his career has developed, McEwan's style has become increasingly realist. He has said in an interview: 'It's enough to try and make some plausible version of what we've got, rather than have characters sprout wings and fly out the window.' What do you think he means by this, and how 'plausible' do you think *Atonement* is?

Part Two is less conventional in structure: after the gradual revelation that the main character – the focaliser – is Robbie; the narrative follows his journey across France with numerous reflections about how he arrived at this point. As such we move back and forth in time and location. Using **free indirect style**, McEwan describes Robbie's first meeting with Cecilia in London after he is released from prison; we also read about Cecilia's life as a probationer nurse in St Thomas' Hospital when she writes to Robbie. But the part has significantly more momentum – and pace – than the previous part and this is, in retrospect, a clear response by Briony to Cyril Connolly's criticism in Part Three that *Two Figures by a Fountain* lacked a 'sense of forward movement'. Parts Two and Three are filled with incident, and have the vital 'pull of simple narrative' that her first – and rejected – effort did not have. The novel's structure, and the style of each part, are an author's attempt at revising a text in the light of criticism.

Part One is the longest and, like Virginia Woolf's work (by which it is influenced), is more concerned with 'the crystalline present' than plot development. Subsequent parts are characterised by journeying, as well as almost obsessive

Free indirect style: (also known as free indirect discourse/ speech) is when the narrator takes on aspects of a character's speech without using inverted commas.

revisions of the past. And so McEwan's structure – loosely tied parts with very different perspectives – is not only artistically coherent and extremely sophisticated, it is also a supremely postmodern text as it challenges the reader's expectations and asks us to question what constitutes a work of fiction. It does so by exposing the craft of writing. For some this is the equivalent of breaking down the fourth wall in drama: it is both liberating and unsettling; for others it breaks an unstated agreement between author and reader and, as a result, takes away much of the pleasure we derive from fiction. The willing suspension of disbelief evaporates when we read Connolly's letter.

Build critical skills

The 'willing suspension of disbelief' is a phrase coined by the poet Samuel Taylor Coleridge (1772–1834). Before researching this, and then applying it to Connolly's letter, what do you think it means in relation to art in general, and specifically to this novel?

CRITICAL VIEW

Read Daniel Zalewski's comment on *Atonement*. How would you explain this 'experiment' to someone who does not know the novel? Discuss this first and then, after reflection, write your explanation in three short paragraphs.

Daniel Zalewski has written:

> More than anything, the structure of 'Atonement' resembles one of those psychological studies which McEwan so admires. If the reader becomes fully invested in the drama – to the point of resenting the revelation that the story is Briony's invention – then, according to McEwan, the experiment worked.

Narrative devices

McEwan's subtle subversion of conventional rules continues in later sections, but we can only begin to fully appreciate them once we have finished reading the novel. For instance, we know from the final section that Briony never meets Robbie and Cecilia in Balham. We suspect that after the wedding she returned to hospital; but her description of herself at the Church as 'a ghostly illuminated apparition', and also as 'the imagined or ghostly persona', adds to our understanding that some of the experiences described are, within this work of fiction itself, fantasy.

Top ten quotation

> Now she had seen him walk across the room, the other possibility, that he could have been killed, seemed outlandish, against all the odds. It would have made no sense … What deliverance.

It is Cyril Connolly's letter in Part Three which is the first clear disruption of the novel's apparent realism. Once we have read this, and understood that Part One of the novel is a novella revised by Briony, our view of the novel is profoundly changed. And it changes still further once we have read the postscript: 'BT London 1999'. We have just read two comparatively consistent and coherent parts, focusing on Robbie Turner and Briony Tallis. There is then a sudden narrative shift in the final part, which is signalled by McEwan's locating it in both time (1999) and place (London).

In fact, it is only when we read the very final line of Part Three that we have to ask ourselves to what extent the story we have just read has a reliable 'narrative arc' of any sort: what actually happened? And how much of it is McEwan's story or Briony's act of atonement? It forces us to think about the role of the narrator in each of the preceding parts: we know of course that McEwan is the author, but is the third-person omniscient narrator Briony? She admits in the final section of the novel that she is 'an unreliable witness' who is capable of creating 'a convenient distortion' if it suits her purpose, but is that the same as an unreliable narrator? And to what extent does her vascular dementia affect her recollection and depiction of the past? We are, of course, supposed to ask such questions of a text that, by its conclusion, has become highly unstable.

Viewpoint

This instability is deliberate and intrinsic to the shifting viewpoints and multiple narrators that we encounter in *Atonement*. Episodes are looked at from different perspectives, often changing how we interpret them.

Most of the novel is written using a third-person omniscient narrator written in the past tense. For much of the novel we assume that this narrator is McEwan: he is the author, these are his characters, and these are the plot lines that he is developing, chapter by chapter. McEwan appears to adopt the viewpoint of a different character for each part of the novel. This is subverted in Part Three when a fictionalised version of Cyril Connolly writes a letter to Briony analysing, effectively, Part One of the novel. It is at this point that the novel changes from a conventional, realist narrative to something much more postmodern.

However, this should not come as a total surprise as there are subtle hints by the author that the story we are reading is a construct: Briony writes that 'six decades later ... how at the age of thirteen she had written her way through a whole history of literature'. There are other moments when the perspective adopted is reflective, rather than fixed in the present. For instance, soon after discovering a distressed Lola, the narrator – we later understand it to be Briony herself – admits that 'she would never be able to console herself that she was pressured or bullied. She never was.' Such a statement is revealing: it prejudices her actions in the eyes of the reader but, later on, gives further insight into Briony's own relationship with her past, and her need for atonement. Such foresights are at odds with a traditional, realist style of writing.

Taking it further ▶▶

Do you think that the shifting perspectives that McEwan employs, coupled with Briony's 'revisions', add to our understanding and enjoyment of *Atonement*, or is the integrity of the text compromised by such an approach? Consider McEwan's aims in constructing the book in this way, and evaluate their success.

TASK

How many episodes in the novel are seen from different viewpoints? To what extent do these affect our interpretation not only of the scene, but also of the characters involved, and the plot?

Setting and atmosphere

Each part of *Atonement* has clearly defined settings: Part One takes place in the Tallis household in rural Surrey in 1935; Part Two is set in Dunkirk in 1940; Part Three is set in London in 1940 and the final part is also set in London, but in 1999. There is a clear narrative arch: the novel begins and ends in the Tallis home, but it spans 64 years and includes chapters set in wartime France and London.

Each setting strongly influences the atmosphere. Part One takes place on the hottest day of the year and this, combined with the claustrophobia of the house, influences characters' behaviour, which in turn shapes the plot. The heatwave that England is sweltering under in Part One is described as 'colossal', 'fierce', 'vast', 'suffocating', 'terrible', which has even 'evaporated' the birdsong of the fields. Leon comments that England during a heatwave is 'a different country' where 'all the rules change'. This breakdown in normality might explain why so many characters appear to behave in irrational ways (Robbie tries to blame his odd behaviour with Cecilia on the heat) but it does not excuse them. That said, the strong sexual charge that exists between Cecilia and Robbie, together with the flirtatious behaviour Lola initially shows to Marshall, seems to be heightened by the heat.

The house is ugly, made of 'bright orange brick' and described as a 'tragedy of wasted chances' (which might also be a subtle reference to the fate of Robbie and Cecilia) and 'charmless to a fault'. It is an imposter, standing in the same place of a more impressive, Adam-style house destroyed by fire in the late 1880s. It was built by Jack Tallis' father, an ironmonger, who specialised in 'padlocks, bolts, latches and hasps'. It is undoubtedly a place of great wealth, complete with extensive grounds, servant quarters, an elaborate fountain and a library. It is a 'solid, secure and functional' place, but is also restrictive and limiting, resembling the prison that Robbie will be sent to, shutting people both in and out of its airless rooms. The overriding atmosphere of this first part of the book is repressive.

Part Two begins in sharp contrast to Part One: instead of rural England we are in wartorn France, and rather than one location there are several, as Robbie tries to find his way to safety (and rescue) in Dunkirk. The atmosphere is intense throughout and the dominant theme is conflict: the war is tearing through Europe, but Robbie is also trying to win battles within himself.

Taking it further ▶▶

Robbie spends much of the novel seeking a place where he can belong: in Part One he is in limbo, moving between his working class roots and the upper-middle class that the Tallis family represent. He then moves between prison and the army. To what extent is his fate a result of him not 'belonging'? And where do you think is his most natural home?

CRITICAL VIEW

Daniel Zalewski, writing in the *New Yorker* magazine has commented that: 'McEwan is a connoisseur of dread, performing the literary equivalent of turning on the tub faucet and leaving the room; the flood is foreseeable, but it still shocks when the water rushes over the edge.' Do what extent is this true of *Atonement*?

Although much of Part Two focuses on France, the scenes described are also punctuated with Robbie's memories and letters from Cecilia (where she describes being a nurse, and also conveys important information about other characters in the novel, including Briony). The setting and atmosphere change over the course of this part, affected by Robbie's injury: what begins with graphic descriptions of war and the effects it has on individuals, ends in the dreamlike, feverish language of a dying man. But what might have been expected to be a tone of great sadness is, instead, something transcendent: Robbie seems to escape from the physical and psychological pain he is in and, for a moment, is reunited with Cecilia, who will wait for him indefinitely. In retrospect we learn that this event has been revised by Briony as she seeks different outcomes to the tragedy she set in motion.

Part Three continues the theme of conflict, but this time on the Home Front. The setting is St Thomas' Hospital in London during 1940, and although the atmosphere is not as unrelentingly intense as Part Two, it does contain moments of almost unbearable agony, both physical and emotional. The hospital's routine, its 'cult of hygiene', is described in great detail by McEwan. We see how the job of becoming a nurse is not only one in which Briony (and Cecilia) learn how to care for others, but is also a process of scrubbing away at one's identity. Briony is reduced to 'N. Tallis' (the N is for Nurse).

The atmosphere is one of waiting: not only for the casualties due to arrive from the Front, but we also wait for Robbie to return and to be reunited with Cecilia. When the men do arrive we see the true human cost of war: those seen as heroes by the public are reduced to vulnerable human beings struggling with overwhelming pain. We learn, with Briony, a 'simple, obvious thing … that a person is, among all else, a material thing, easily torn, not easily mended'. The atmosphere turns from waiting to something closer to the intensity of Part Two.

After the war there is the peace of the final part. The setting is, once again, London, but we are at the end of the twentieth century, and the atmosphere is very much one of reflection and calm. There is also a melancholy air as Briony learns that her 'brain, her mind, is closing down' as a result of vascular dementia. The opening sentence of this section is: 'what a strange time this has been', and this strangeness is about to become more pronounced for the reader as the novel's workings are further revealed. And in order for the novel's structure to work, and for us to realise that the 'author' is Briony, this part has to be written in the first person. London 1999, then, also marks the (very self-aware) end of the main character's life. This is 'part of the reluctant process of letting go' for the 77-year-old Briony, an opportunity to make 'a tidy finish':

> Displace, transmute, dissemble. Bring down the fogs of
> the imagination!

But of course for the reader the ending is far from 'tidy': we realise that what we have just read is 'a convenient distortion'. The characters who have survived from earlier parts, although all elderly, are 'exactly the same' for Briony. Or

Build critical skills

Which part do you think gives us the more accurate representation of the true horror of war – Part Two or Part Three? Pick out images and episodes to support your points.

at least they appear to be, but we cannot be certain: is Mr Nettle who helps Briony with her research the Corporal Nettle from Part Two, or has she simply borrowed this name for her fiction? We do not know. But such ambiguity is part of the narrative: she admits that she makes 'typos', but that also she is 'good at not thinking about the things that are really troubling me', a statement which appears to make little sense. What might appear to be atmosphere of calm could instead be the early onset of dementia; where there were once words are now gaps; where there were memories are now dreams conjured up for the sake of atonement.

The final part brings us full circle: back to the Tallis home, and Briony admits this to herself:

> As into the sunset we sail. An unhappy inversion. It occurs to me that I have not travelled so very far after all, since I wrote my little play. Or rather, I've made a huge digression and doubled back to my starting place.

The novel ends with hope, but it is self-delusional. Briony admits that the 'real' ending, which would have described Robbie dying of septicaemia and Cecilia being killed in the London Blitz, could have been written 'in the service of the bleakest realism'. The ending is as much a fantasy as *The Trials of Arabella*, both complete with princes (in the play there is the 'gorgeous prince', and in this final section we have a 'medical prince'), both telling a tale of love surviving against all the odds. Briony 'no longer possesses the courage of [her] pessimism': she rewrites the narrative to protect both her and her readers from the painful 'truth'.

Choice of language (including imagery)

The author Zadie Smith has written:

> *McEwan's prose is controlled, careful, and powerfully concise; he is eloquent on the subjects of sex and sexuality; he has a strong head for the narrative possibilities of science; his novels are no longer than is necessary; he would never write a sentence featuring this many semicolons. When I read him I am struck by metaphors I would never think to use, plots that don't occur to me, ideas I have never had. I love to read him for these reasons and also because, like his millions of readers, I feel myself to be in safe hands. Picking up a book by McEwan is to know, at the very least, that what you read therein will be beautifully written, well-crafted, and not an embarrassment, either for you or for him.*

Ian McEwan has said that his style 'is shaped by the novel I am writing; it's very much driven by the material itself'. Understanding this is crucial to appreciating McEwan's choice of language in *Atonement*. Once we realise that Briony is the primary 'author' of the book – rather than McEwan – then not only does our interpretation of events change but so does our appreciation of the

▲ Zadie Smith

language used. What makes it more complex is that Briony's style in turn has also been shaped by different writers: in his rejection letter to her, Cyril Connolly comments on how much Briony's story has been influenced by 'the techniques of Mrs Woolf'. Connolly also admits that the novelist Elizabeth Bowen has read the manuscript and this in turn could have influenced not only the revised style of the novella, but also the subject matter (one of Bowen's novels – *The Demon Lover* – tells the story of a dead soldier who returns to wartorn London to be reunited with his lover).

> ## TASK
> Elizabeth Bowen is seldom read now, but do some research on her and consider how justified McGrath's description is of Part One. Read *The Heat of the Day*, as well as looking online for articles about her (keyterms could be Elizabeth Bowen + war + fiction).

McEwan claims that he likes 'a careful, fairly precise prose, I like to use imagery sparingly so that when it is there I hope it will be all the more vivid'. However, as we have seen, this technique can be deliberately adapted to ensure that the novel is artistically coherent. Reading Connolly's letter in which he criticises *Two Figures by a Fountain* for a lack of pace, partially explains the intensity of the writing in Part Two when, it could be argued, there is a surfeit of powerful images, ranging from a child's leg caught in the branches of a tree, to horses being routinely shot by a French officer.

McEwan's prose in this part is unsparing in its depiction of violence. For him, 'if violence is simply there to excite it's merely pornographic.' He argues that 'if you're going to have [violence], you've got to show it in all its horror.'

For McEwan, 'language will generate the plot' and it is perhaps in *Atonement* that this is most clearly visible: this is a novel about writing, and the choice of words tell us much about the characters and the storylines, but also – by extension – the 'author' herself. As she writes and revises, so is the plot revised, until we are left with a number of different plotlines that are resolved – or not – by her choice of endings.

Some of the criticism levelled at *Atonement* stem from McEwan's structure and concentration on language: events which would have deepened our understanding of the characters and their fates (such as Robbie's trial, his years in prison or Cecilia's rejection of her family) are either omitted entirely or glossed over by McEwan. Furthermore, once we realise that Robbie's 'story' in Part Two has been largely invented by Briony, some readers might feel that their emotions have been manipulated by McEwan: the intensity of the prose is lessened when we realise in the final part that this has been researched by Briony, rather than actually experienced by Robbie. All this could be explained by Briony's unwillingness to develop and reveal events that are too painful for

> ## CRITICAL VIEW
> The critic Charles McGrath has written: 'the first part of the book in particular, with its child's-eye point of view, its slow, meticulous descriptions of the Tallis country house, is so Bowen-like as almost to be pastiche.'

> ## TASK
> At the start of his career McEwan gained the nickname of 'Ian Macabre' because of the explicit descriptions of violence. To what extent would you agree with McEwan's view of how violence is described in art? Does a writer have a moral duty to show it as honestly as possible, or should the audience be protected from it?

her as a character *and* author, and this has artistic coherence, but we are left asking if it also denies the reader a more complete understanding of 'what *really* happened'.

Build critical skills

Reflecting on the structure of *Atonement* McEwan has said: 'I'm still often asked, "What really happened?" … I don't tire of it, because I think that to ask that question of me means I succeeded in something.' What 'something' do you think he has succeeded in?

Contexts

Target your thinking

- How can setting *Atonement* within a broad range of contexts deepen your understanding of the text and the ways in which different readers might respond to it? (**AO3**)
- What links might be traced between *Atonement* and various other literary texts? (**AO4**)
- How can applying various critical approaches enrich your understanding of *Atonement* and the ways in which different readers might interpret it? (**AO5**)

Biographical context

Ian McEwan was born on 21 June 1948 in Aldershot, England. He studied English Literature at the University of Sussex, graduating in 1970. He completed an MA in Creative Writing in the University of East Anglia. His father, David, was a working-class Scot who eventually became a major in the British army. Much of McEwan's early life was spent living in Germany and Libya before joining a state boarding school in Suffolk. McEwan has talked at length about being sent away from home, and how it forced him to reflect on his own identity. He was aware from an early age of how one thinks and makes sense of the world, and this is reflected in Part One of *Atonement*. He said in an interview:

> *The moment in 'Atonement' when Briony is crooking her finger and wondering at which point the intention is actually resolved into a movement is something very much from my childhood.*

After university McEwan moved to London in 1974, where he started contributing to literary magazines such as *The New Review* and the *Times Literary Supplement*. He soon became established as a member of an influential group of young writers (which included Julian Barnes, Martin Amis and Christopher Hitchens). McEwan's early writing was characterised by its dark – and often macabre – subject matter. His first collection of short stories, *First Love, Last Rites*, was published in 1975 and won the Somerset Maugham Award. His second collection, *In Between the Sheets*, was published in 1978, again to much critical acclaim. His first novel, *The Cement Garden*, also published in 1978, is perhaps his most gruesome work and focuses on murder and incest (he gained the nickname 'Ian Macabre' in the media). His next novel, *The Comfort of Strangers*, published in 1981, was shortlisted for the Booker Prize.

▲ Ian McEwan

He has published novels regularly throughout his career, often winning awards. *The Child in Time*, published in 1987, won the Whitbread Novel Award. It remains one of his most popular and powerful works, and moved further away from the themes that dominated his early writing. Other novels he has published include *The Innocent* (1990), *Black Dogs* (1992) and *Enduring Love* (1997), which was made into a successful film in 2004 starring Daniel Craig. *Amsterdam*, published in 1998, won the Booker Prize. *Saturday* was published in 2005; *On Chesil Beach*, a novella, in 2007 and was shortlisted for the Booker Prize; *Solar* was published in 2010 and *Sweet Tooth* in 2012. His latest novel, *The Children Act*, was published in 2014.

Atonement was published in 2001 and is perhaps his most popular novel; it was made into a critically acclaimed film, starring Keira Knightley and James McAvoy, in 2007. In addition to writing books, McEwan has written plays for television and film scripts, including *The Ploughman's Lunch* in 1985. He lives in London with his second wife.

Many themes and techniques explored in *Atonement* can be found in other novels by McEwan: the fascination for childhood is there in *The Cement Garden* and *The Child in Time*; psychological trauma and depression are very much in evidence in *Black Dogs*; the unreliable narrator is a key feature in *Enduring Love*, and justice is at the core of *The Children Act*. It is worth reading some of these other works to get a more secure understanding of McEwan's style, and his interpretation of human nature. In doing so one can gain a greater insight into *Atonement*.

Literary context

The roots of *Atonement* lie in the work of a number of different writers. Some are named in the novel (for example, Virginia Woolf, Elizabeth Bowen and Cyril Connolly), while others can be felt more subtly through the influence of their ideas or style (for example, the broken vase in Part One is an allusion to the broken gilded crystal bowl in Henry James' novel *The Golden Bowl*). McEwan has said that Jane Austen 'is crucial to this novel', and knowing this helps us to comprehend the ambition behind *Atonement*. The epigraph is taken from Austen's *Northanger Abbey* (published in 1818): it refers to the 'dreadful nature' of Catherine Morland's (the heroine) invented secrets about General Tilney (Tilney's is of course the name of the Tallis home-turned-hotel of the final part). In Austen's novel, Catherine's fantasies are exposed, much to her disgrace. *Northanger Abbey* is a novel preoccupied with the conflict between imagination and reality, and the consequences that occur when the two are confused and long-established laws are challenged, sometimes out of ignorance. In an interview McEwan said:

I wanted to play with the notion of storytelling as a form of self-justification, of how much courage is involved in telling the truth to oneself. What are the distances between what is real and what is imagined? Catherine Morland … was a girl so full of the delights of Gothic fiction that she causes havoc around her when she imagines a perfectly innocent man to be capable of the most terrible things … I've been thinking how I might devise a hero or heroine who could echo that process in Catherine Morland, but then go a step further and look at, not the crime, but the process of atonement, and do it through … storytelling.

There are many other allusions to other writers: for example, in Part One Cecilia and Robbie discuss Samuel Richardson's novel *Clarissa*. Richardson is widely believed to be the first English novelist, but he began making money from writing love letters for his friends at thirteen – Briony's age at the start of the novel. The eponymous heroine of Richardson's novel has a sister called Arabella (the name of Briony's own heroine in her melodrama). More importantly, *Clarissa* is an epistolary novel which provides a number of different viewpoints on events: as we can see, letters and different perspectives are central to the structure of McEwan's novel.

The most direct 'intervention' by a writer occurs in Part Three when Briony receives a rejection letter from Cyril Connolly, editor of *Horizon* magazine. This parody very accurately captures Connolly's personality: well known for socialising (he invites Briony to join him for a glass of wine), famously cultured and well travelled (his letter ranges across literature, art and politics), but also not without some inherited prejudices (he assumes that Briony is either a doctor, or a patient). Connolly's letter also forces the reader to revaluate *Atonement*. It is not a traditional, linear narrative: instead, through the inclusion of this letter it has become transformed into a **metafictional** postmodernist work: it has deliberately challenged our preconceptions of what a conventional novel should do.

Connolly's advice is clearly accepted by Briony, and we can see the changes between the novella she has sent him and the story we have read. For example, the vase is no longer Ming (Connolly claims it should be something less expensive); the Bernini fountain is in the Piazza Barberini not, as Briony has originally written, in the Piazza Navona. Such changes reveal the artifice behind the art, forcing us to think about what is 'fiction' and what is not.

Atonement, then, is a novel about a writer and writing, and these are subjects that McEwan returns to regularly in his work, employing writers as characters to explore complex ideas about the imagination and the differences between reality and fiction. But, beyond this, the novel's structure challenges the reader not only to think about the truth of what they have read, but also to re-evaluate the characters, plot and reliability of the narrator when the mechanics of the creative act are revealed.

Metafiction is literature which self-consciously refers to, and draws attention to, its own construction by departing from the conventions of its genre.

▲ Cyril Connolly, a well-known literary figure. How does including a real person in the novel change our perspective?

Historical context

For Ian McEwan, the Second World War is integral to his own identity: he was born in 1948 and his father was a professional soldier. He says:

> *The war shaped our family life. It was the war that brought my parents together. It was the war that killed my mother's first husband. I grew up in army camps in places in the world in which, again, our presence was to some extent determined by the recent war. [The war] was a constant presence.*

War is present in each part of *Atonement*. At the top of the social hierarchy, Jack Tallis is involved in British rearmament to combat German aggression, and even Paul Marshall is indirectly involved in preparations for war through his manufacturing of the Amo bar. Lower down that hierarchy, there are rumours that Robbie's father left home to fight in the First World War, and Danny Hardman is killed at sea during the Second World War. All classes, young and old, women and men, rural and urban, are affected by war. Even in the final section of the novel war is present in the scenes set in the Imperial War Museum: its consequences reach back and forward in time.

The two parts in the novel set during the war have a narrative momentum deliberately missing from Part One, as both Robbie and Briony are driven forward on their own journeys towards their own fates. The many descriptions of death and violence are deliberately graphic because, for McEwan 'either you *do* violence or you sentimentalise it'. The retreat from Dunkirk has been written into British political history as a heroic victory, but it was a defeat that cost the lives of thousands of soldiers and civilians, and McEwan's aim was to attempt to reveal its true horror. Clearly, in *Atonement* actions have consequences: the shrapnel that kills Robbie, the casualties that Briony has to try to help, are the imagined realities of war.

Although the Second World War dominates *Atonement*, its historical reach of the novel extends beyond the Europe of 1940. We see how events are linked, and that they continue to resonate after they have happened, affecting the present and influencing the future. For example, Uncle Clem's vase – which plays such a pivotal part in the plot – is a family heirloom, but its importance lies in being a gift to him from the people of Verdun for rescuing their village from the German forces. The vase becomes symbolic of a number of things – virginity, the fragility of life, the conflict between appearance and reality – but it also links generations and different conflicts.

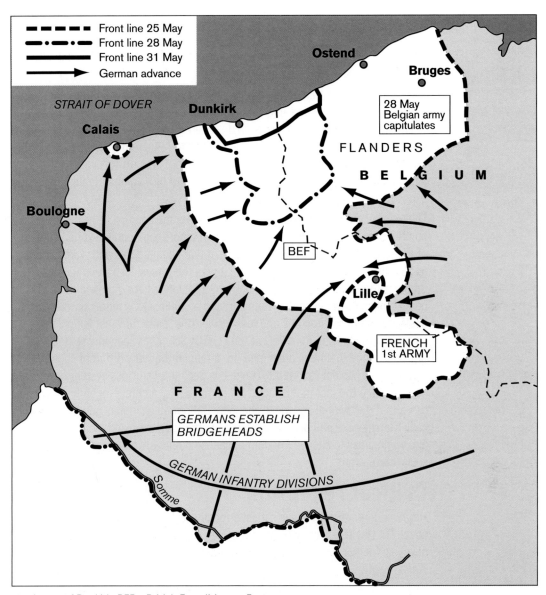

Front line 25 May
Front line 28 May
Front line 31 May
German advance

STRAIT OF DOVER

Ostend

Bruges

28 May
Belgian army
capitulates

Dunkirk

Calais

FLANDERS

B E L G I U M

Boulogne

BEF

Lille

FRENCH
1st ARMY

F R A N C E

GERMANS ESTABLISH
BRIDGEHEADS

GERMAN INFANTRY DIVISIONS

Somme

▲ A map of Dunkirk. BEF = British Expeditionary Force

Social and cultural contexts

Atonement explores the transformation of women's roles in England between
1935 and 1999. There are many examples of institutional prejudice in Part One.
For example, although both Cecilia and Robbie studied English at Cambridge,
it is Robbie who flourishes. Emily is critical of her daughter's desire to study
English, and although women were allowed to attend lectures they were
regarded by many colleges as second-class citizens. Indeed, some colleges

only allowed women to graduate with certain degrees from 1948. Emily Tallis has no independent career of her own, and is dismissive of Cecilia's education, regarding it as an indulgence. Other female characters in Part One include Betty and Grace Turner, both of whom are servants.

The central act that transforms the lives of every character is a rape – the ultimate act of male abuse and subjugation of a woman – and the reactions of each character once this has been discovered is a skilful analysis of social preconceptions of the time. The England that the Tallis family occupy is represented as claustrophobic and inward-looking: the petty prejudices that allow them to neglect the Quincey children and to turn against Robbie are subtly exposed by McEwan.

The war forced significant social changes across the country. Only a small number of professions were open to women before the Second World War (one of them being nursing), but the outbreak of war changed this and women began to fill jobs left vacant by men who had joined the forces. Like many women, Briony is forced to grow up very quickly in a society where old certainties are being broken down. In contrast the England of 1999 seems more content with itself: it is more meritocratic and less insular (the 'cheerful West Indian' taxi-driver is also studying for a PhD at the London School of Economics). It is, like the Tallis home that he is driving her to, a familiar but very different country, and one that has not resorted to 'tasteless decline'. The class system *has* declined, and the fact that Briony's old home is now a hotel – open to all who can afford it – symbolises these changes. But not all change is good: Lord and Lady Marshall are still alive and more powerful than ever, and their wealth and willingness to silence freedom of speech points to continuing elements of social corruption.

Critical reception

Atonement remains McEwan's most critically acclaimed and well-received novel. For David Sexton, writing in the *Evening Standard*, it 'is McEwan's best novel, so far, his masterpiece'; Michiko Kakutani, reviewing it in the *New York Times*, wrote:

> *'Atonement' emerges as the author's most deeply felt novel yet … It is novel that attests not only to Mr. McEwan's mastery of craft and virtuosic control of narrative suspense, but also to his knowledge of the human heart and its rage for symmetry and order.*

Its reception was no less enthusiastic among academics. Frank Kermode, Professor of English Literature at Cambridge University, felt that the novel lives 'on that borderline between fantasy and fact that is indeed the territory of fiction'. For Kermode it was 'easily his finest'. Hermione Lee, Professor of English Literature at Oxford University, described the novel as 'impressive, engrossing, deep and surprising'. The novel's reputation was, if anything, further enhanced when the film adaptation was released in 2008, again to great critical acclaim. Directed by Joe Wright, and starring Keira Knightley, James McAvoy and Benedict Cumberbatch, it received many nominations and awards around the world, including a BAFTA and a Golden Globe for best film.

TASK

Watch the movie adaptation and consider some of the differences between the text and screen: which work, and which do not? Consider the success of the Dunkirk scenes, and evaluate how successfully the film-maker conveys the revelation that Robbie and Cecilia are never reunited but die apart.

Working with the text

Assessment Objectives and skills

> **AO1** Articulate informed, personal and creative responses to literary texts, using associated concepts and terminology, and coherent, accurate written expression.

This AO rewards your essay-writing skills. You need to show:

◄ quality of argument

◄ organisation of ideas

◄ use of appropriate concepts and terminology

◄ technical accuracy.

You need to decide on your main ideas and your approach before you start to write your answer. You should write fluently and accurately, structuring your essay carefully, linking your paragraphs, guiding your reader clearly through your line of argument and using the sophisticated vocabulary, including critical terminology, which is appropriate to an A-level essay. You will need to use frequent embedded quotations to give evidence of close detailed knowledge, and you should demonstrate familiarity with the whole text.

> **AO2** Analyse ways in which meanings are shaped in literary texts.

It is expected that students pay close attention to the methods used by writers to achieve their effects, and use detailed and accurate quotations to support their points. Students may focus on relevant aspects of:

◄ form and genre

◄ narrative structure

◄ language, tone, imagery, and so on.

> **AO3** Demonstrate understanding of the significance and influence of the contexts in which literary texts are written and received.

Whether your essay deals with a single text or compares two or more texts, the examiner expects students to address the central issue of the question, as well as show understanding of a range of relevant contexts: some regarding the production of the texts at the time of writing, others exploring how the texts have been received over time and, most importantly of all in this specification, contexts for how the texts can be interpreted by readers now.

> **AO4** Explore connections across literary texts.

In a comparative essay, you should try to find specific points of comparison, rather than merely generalising. You will find it easier to make connections between texts (of any kind) if you try to balance them as you write; remember also that connections are not only about finding similarities – differences are just as interesting. Above all, think about how consider how the comparison illuminates each text; some connections will be thematic, others generic or stylistic.

> **AO5** Explore literary texts informed by different interpretations.

For this AO, you can refer to the opinions of critics, but you should also be alert to aspects of the novel which are open to interpretation. Your job is to measure your own interpretation of the text against those of other readers.

Individual text information

Atonement is currently set by the following examination boards:

AQA English Literature A A-level	A-level Paper: 'Love through the ages'. Written examination; 3 hours; open book, clean text; in Section C only; 75 marks; 40% of A-level
AQA English Literature B A-level	A-level Paper 2: 'Texts and genres'. Written examination; 3 hours; open book, clean text; 75 marks; 40% of A-level
OCR English Literature A Level	Literature post-1900 (Non-examined assessment component); suggested text for texts grouped under the theme of 'Time'
Edexcel English Literature A level	A level Component 2: Prose. Written examination; 1 hour; open book, clean copies; 40 marks; 20% of A level; suggested text for 'Childhood' (post-1900 text)

For **AQA Specification A**, *Atonement* is set as an examined text at A-level paper, on the theme of **'Love through the ages'**. For both papers, the novel must be studied in conjunction with another text. It must be compared with at least two poems from the **Anthology of Love Poetry: pre-1900.**

The A-level paper is three hours long; there are three questions, each being marked out of 25, so there is one hour allocated for this essay.

The aim of 'Love through the ages' is to 'encourage students to explore aspects of a central literary theme as seen over time, using unseen material and set texts.' The best preparation for this topic is to read as much as possible around the subject, ensuring that as many different authors, and periods, are explored.

In doing so students will have a stronger grasp of the many similar plot lines, and themes, that have dominated this topic over time.

During this period of reading students should endeavour to try to make connections within – and across – texts. There should be a focus on how authors shape meaning, and how this meaning is influenced by a number of factors, most obviously including the historical context the text was written in. It can be extremely rewarding to research how each text was received at the time of publication, and to also look at its on-going critical reception. Different interpretations of well-established texts – such as those by historicist or feminist critics – may also prove thought-provoking. It is particularly important with this specification that students show a secure understanding of how the texts selected can be received by readers today. Understanding that texts and their meanings are not fixed is also an important factor in this topic.

'Love through the ages' is a complex topic and it is impossible to provide a definitive list of aspects for students to study. However, an awareness of the various representations of love should include: romantic love; love and sex; the social conventions that surround love; how love, and its representation, changes through the ages; love and loss (including the loss of a lover through separation and death); the effect that jealousy can have on love; marriage, children, divorce and old age.

For **AQA Specification B**, *Atonement* is set as an examined text for A-level only, as part of Paper 2, '**Texts and genres: elements of crime writing**'. Questions are set on individual texts. The paper is three hours long and each question is awarded 25 marks; 60 minutes should be spent on each essay.

Many of the texts in 'Elements of crime writing' pre-date the crime fiction genre that became increasingly popular in the mid-nineteenth century. However, all the texts share common elements: a significant crime is at the centre of the plot, and the consequences of the crime influence how the rest of the narrative develops.

Additionally, all the set texts contain subversive elements that challenge established orders. These challenges might be directed at national, social, religious and moral laws, or they might be more complex, and less obvious (for example, challenging modes of behaviour with certain social classes). Students need to keep in mind the many 'elements' that could be explored in the text, including;

- ◤ the nature of the crime, whether it is a straightforward detective story, or a post-modern narrative
- ◤ the moral dimension to 'crime', including the extent to which the reader is asked to empathise with the criminal
- ◤ the extent that the settings influence the actions of the characters, and the crimes committed

- the crimes themselves, the motives behind them
- the possible use of violence, and murder, in the crimes
- the physical and psychological effects the crimes have on all characters, including the victims and criminals; an analysis of suffering could be explored
- the creation of the stereotypical detective hero
- the means by which the detective sets about solving the crime
- the relationship between the criminal and the detective hero, and the extent to which they are both similar and different (both morally and behaviourally)
- the nature of the investigation that leads to the capture of the criminal
- the criminal's 'confession', and the acceptance (or rejection) of responsibility and guilt for the crimes caused; the need for forgiveness
- the punishment of the criminal: this could expose the strengths and failings of various forms of justice, including a society's legal system, as well as more abstract systems (such as fate, or divine justice)
- the aftermath of the crimes, and the restoration of order that comes with this catharsis
- themes and motifs that develop out of the crime, such as love, betrayal, jealousy, sex and death
- the depiction of the various manifestations of the legal system, including criminal trials, courtroom dramas, gangland subculture, prisons, police teams
- the structure of the text as it develops through a series of incidents to the final climax where the criminal is exposed and the crime solved
- a clear focus on plot
- the use of language associated with law and crime: this might include legal terminology and jargon, to the informal registers used by police and criminals. Equally, such preconceived ideas about how different elements of society speak can be challenged by the author
- the use of crime writing as a method of exposing both strengths and weaknesses in a society at a given point in history
- how crime stories affect readers, establishing suspense, excitement, and enjoyment.

Although *Atonement* is not typical of this genre, a crime is committed (by Briony, but also by Marshall) and the author explores justice and forgiveness. How it subverts the genre is also an important part of its narrative development.

Meeting the Assessment Objectives

AO1	Articulate informed, personal and creative responses to literary texts, using associated concepts and terminology, and coherent, accurate written expression.

Practise writing timed essays by hand, so that your writing remains legible and you are accustomed to shaping your essay within the specified time. Take care not to go over time or the other answers will suffer. Do not start writing straight away, even if other candidates do: spend around 25% of your time thinking and planning. If you take time to plan your answer, your essay will be more coherent and your line of argument easier to follow. Examiners appreciate succinct, legible essays which guide the reader through to a carefully planned conclusion. Select your main material and plan your approach before you start to write, and always write a concluding paragraph, even if you are running out of time.

AO2	Analyse ways in which meanings are shaped in literary texts.

For **form**, you need to demonstrate an understanding of what McEwan achieves by his use of multiple perspectives and different narrative voices. We initially read the text as a conventional third-person realist narrative, but this changes, and there are moments when this moves closer to free indirect style more appropriate to a postmodernist text. Different voices contribute to this effect: McEwan himself of course, but also Briony, and letters (variously) written by Robbie, Cecilia and a fictionalised version of the writer and critic Cyril Connolly. Each shift in emphasis and perspective contributes to the novel's evolving form, culminating in the final section which reveals the extent to which the previous pages have been invented by the main narrator to explain her actions, and provide a less bleak ending.

The **structure** of *Atonement* is intrinsic to its effectiveness. Each of its four parts are distinct, but not immediately and obviously linked. What links them all is Briony, but this only becomes obvious in the final part, and indeed it could be argued that it is only by reading the very final words of Part Three ('BT London 1999') and then linking these with the next part, that we fully understand how much each section has been revised by the narrator. Showing an awareness of *the whole text* throughout your essay is important: you should show that you clearly understand how each part of this intricately complex novel depends on the other if it is be fully understood.

Ian McEwan is renowned for his precise use of **language**: for him it is more important than plot. However, in this novel there are changes in his use of language in a number of different areas and, once again, this is linked to structure. Part One is the longest section in the novel and it is deliberately lacking in the pace of subsequent parts. In this sense it is clearly (and deliberately) influenced by Virginia Woolf's writing style (and is criticised by Cyril Connolly for this). Briony makes some revisions to the text in light of his criticisms, and we can assume that Parts Two and Three, filled with incidents and containing much overtly shocking imagery, is also a direct response to Connolly's letter.

In order to obtain high marks in this AO, you should practise writing analytical sentences, comprising a brief quotation or close reference, a definition, or description of the feature you intend to analyse, an explanation of how McEwan has used this feature, and an evaluation of why he chose it, but not necessarily in that order:

Definition	Explanation	Quotation	Evaluation
The vase is a complex symbol.	It represents many things, including the Tallis family, innocence and virginity.	Like Robbie's and Cecilia's relationship, once broken it lies there, 'apart, writhing in the broken light'.	An image that conveys physical and psychological agony.

> **AO3** Demonstrate understanding of the significance and influence of the contexts in which literary texts are written and received.

It is not knowledge of the contexts that is rewarded here, so do not write a lot of contextual material. The examiners are looking for an understanding of the influence of a range of contexts. For *Atonement* some **awareness** of the effect of England in the mid-1930s, as well as the Second World War, is essential here, as well as an **understanding** of some of the key episodes described in the novel (such as the retreat from Dunkirk and the effect that the war was having on the Home Front).

Another relevant area to research would be the changing role of women in the society of the time: look at how Cecilia's experiences at Cambridge differ from Robbie's. Also consider how different – and similar – are male and female experiences of the war: Robbie, Cecilia and Briony are on very different 'front lines', and have very different experiences. There are, however, overlaps, and the parallels between soldiering and nursing are much in evidence. Class is also a factor in this novel: it could be argued that Robbie is found guilty of rape because he does not have the innate sense of privilege and power that Marshall has. Class is also in evidence in the Tallis household, where characters such as the Hardmans and Betty are almost passive observers of the action of their 'masters'. Compare this with London in 1999, a much more meritocratic society seemingly at ease with itself.

For **Edexcel**, Pre-1900 texts are Henry James' *What Maisie Knew*, Charles Dickens' *Hard Times*; and Post-1900 texts are Ian McEwan's *Atonement*, Ailce Walker's *The Color Purple*. Students are required to either:

◄ Compare how writers from your two chosen texts develop tension in the family. OR

◄ Compare how the writers from your two chosen texts explore their characters' internal lives.

For both answers students are advised to relate their analysis to appropriate contextual factors. Each question holds a total of 40 marks.

> **AO4** Explore connections across literary texts.

For **AQA Specification B**, which offers single text questions, you would be rewarded in discussing, when appropriate, the influence of the many writers referred to in the novel. Jane Austen (*Northanger Abbey*), Henry James (*The Golden Bowl*) and Elizabeth Bowen (*The Heat of the Day*) are clearly strong influences on the symbolism and imagery of *Atonement*. However, many other writers are also alluded to: Virginia Woolf, W.H. Auden, W.B. Yeats, Shakespeare (*Twelfth Night*), D.H. Lawrence (*Lady Chatterley's Lover*), Samuel Richardson (*Clarissa*). The list is long and you should refer to them only when appropriate. Of perhaps more significance is showing a clear knowledge and understanding of Cyril Connolly and *Horizon*, the magazine he edited between 1940 and 1950: his rejection letter directly influences Briony's writing style. Study his letter, and research the considerable influence he and *Horizon* had at the time, in order to gain a secure grasp of this important aspect of the novel.

For **Edexcel** and **AQA Specification A**, both boards expect that, in connecting their two texts, students will address the central issue of the question as an important factor when considering the theme of love in texts which are written a substantial period apart. Students might focus on:

◄ similarity and/or difference at the level of subject matter

◄ similarity and/or difference at the level of the ways in which writers present their thoughts and opinions about the issue in the question

◄ the extent to which each text's representation of the issue and its relationship to love can be seen as typical of the genre or its historical period.

To prepare for this, find direct points of comparison and contrast that you may be able to call on in the exam.

> **AO5** Explore literary texts informed by different interpretations.

To fulfil the demands of this Assessment Objective, you can refer to the opinions of critics and/or you can explore different interpretations that you can offer from your own reading of the novel.

McEwan is a contemporary author who has been interviewed many times, not only about *Atonement* but also about his influences and writing style. Many of these are available online, both in printed sources and in filmed talks and interviews he has given at literary events. It is worth consulting these as you study the text. Perhaps more than any other novel he has written, *Atonement* has divided readers and critics: its radical, postmodernist subversion of the conventional realist narrative has been mostly hailed as a great success, but some felt that it broke an unwritten agreement between the author and his reader that weakened the text irretrievably. Because we do not know 'what really happens', constructing a meaningful and coherent analysis becomes even more difficult for the student. Acknowledging such difficulties is necessary because they are deliberate and integral to the structure of the novel.

This is a novel about writing, and about both interpretation and misinterpretation. As such you should show a clear understanding of how different events are observed from different perspectives, each with their own understanding of what happens. There is, in this novel, no definitive and final description of what happens, and even on the final page Briony hints that *another* redraft is possible. Meaning, then, is unfixed, and the words themselves unstable. Recognising the importance of such techniques and exploring how they are deployed by McEwan will help you gain high marks in this AO.

Building skills 1: Structuring your writing

This section focuses upon organising your written responses to convey your ideas as clearly and effectively as possible: the 'how' of your writing as opposed to the 'what'. More often than not, if your knowledge and understanding of *Atonement* is sound, a disappointing mark or grade will be down to one of two common mistakes: misreading the question or failing to organise your response economically and effectively. In an examination you'll be lucky if you can demonstrate 5 per cent of what you know about *Atonement*; luckily, if it's the right 5 per cent, that's all you need to gain full marks.

Understanding your examination

It is important to prepare for the specific type of response your examination body sets with regard to *Atonement*. You will almost certainly know whether you are studying the novel as part of a **non-examined assessment unit** (i.e. for coursework) or as an **examination set text** – but you also need to know if your paper is **open book** – i.e. you will have a clean copy of the text available to you in the exam, or **closed book**, in which case you will not. You really need to find out about this, because the format of your assessment has important implications for the way you organise your response, and dictates the depth and detail required to achieve a top band mark.

Open book

In an open book exam when you have a copy of *Atonement* on the desk in front of you, there can be no possible excuse for failing to quote relevantly, accurately and extensively. To gain a high mark, you are expected to focus in detail on specific passages. Remember, too, that you must not refer to any supporting material such as the Introduction Notes contained within the set edition of your text. If an examiner suspects that you have been lifting chunks of unacknowledged material from such a source, they will refer your paper to the examining body for possible plagiarism.

Closed book

In a closed book exam, because the examiner is well aware that you do not have your text in front of you, their expectations will be different. While you are still expected to support your argument with relevant quotations, close textual references are also encouraged and rewarded. Again, since you will have had to memorise quotations, slight inaccuracies will not be severely punished. Rather than a forensically detailed analysis of a specific section of *Atonement*, the examiner will expect you to range more broadly across the play to structure your response.

Non-examined assessment (NEA)

Writing about *Atonement* within a non-examined assessment unit (i.e. coursework) context poses a very different set of challenges from an examination, in that incorrect quotations and disorientating arguments are liable to cost you much more dearly. Your essay must be wholly and consistently relevant to the title selected; there is no excuse for going off track if you or your teacher have mapped out the parameters of your chosen topic in the first place.

Step 1: Planning and beginning: locate the debate

A very common type of exam question invites you to open up a debate about the text by using various trigger words and phrases such as **'consider the view that …'**, **'some readers think that …'** or **'how far do you agree with this view?'** When analysing this type of question, the one thing you can be sure of is that exam questions never offer a view that makes no sense at all, or one so blindingly obvious that all anyone can do is agree with it; there will always be a genuine interpretation at stake. Similarly, many NEA tasks are written to include a stated view to help give some shape to your writing, so logically your introduction needs to address the terms of this debate and sketch out the outlines of how you intend to move the argument forward to orientate the reader. Since it is obviously going to be helpful if you know this before you start writing, you really do need to plan before you begin to write.

Undertaking a lively debate about some of the ways in which *Atonement* has been and can be interpreted is the DNA of your essay. Of course, any good argument needs to be honest, but to begin by writing 'yes, I totally agree with this obviously true statement' suggests a fundamental misunderstanding of what studying literature is all about. Any stated view in an examination question is designed to open up critical conversations, not shut them down.

Plan your answer by collecting together points for and against the given view. Aim to see a stated opinion as an interesting way of focusing upon a key facet of *Atonement*, like the following student.

Student A

This student is studying AQA English Literature B. The question she is answering is:

'Although Briony does commit a crime it is not the greatest one in the novel: McEwan shows that is the crime of war'.

To what extent do you agree with this view? Remember to include detailed explorations of McEwan's authorial methods in your answer.

Although 'Atonement' (2001) features many scenes set during World War II it could be argued that the author's main aim is to show the effect that the wider theme of conflict has on individuals and families. The two parts principally concerned with war (Parts Two and Three) are framed by two parts set in peace time: Part One is set in 1935 (when tensions in Europe are already growing) and London in 1999. But what is common to all four parts is that psychological, emotional, as well as physical conflict, dominate the characters' experiences. Each come to make sense of the world through painful events. Set against this context Briony's crime appears to be relatively unimportant.

'Atonement' contains many crimes. Marshall's sexual assault on Lola is perhaps the most obvious, but there are other, more psychological 'crimes': the Quincey children are described as 'refugees from a bitter domestic civil war', and even Briony acts violently as she dreams of killing her cousins after they ruin her play's performance. There are many more examples. Of course, the main focus of this part of the novel is Marshall's attack on Lola, but to some extent this is secondary to the consequences that develop after it. No crime exists in a vacuum.

McEwan does not flinch in showing every crime creates a series of consequences. Apparently unimportant disagreements have serious implications: for example, the breaking of the vase in Part One — which is a direct result of Cecilia and Robbie arguing — sets in train a series of events that result in Robbie being sentenced to jail and, eventually, dying of septicaemia in France. Internal, psychological conflict is also fundamental to understanding this novel: Briony's long process of realising the seriousness of her crime, and her need for atonement, dominates Part Three and London 1999, as does Robbie's journeying — both physical and emotional — in Part Two. Crime, then, can be interpreted in a number of different ways.

Part Two of the novel is, for many, the most powerful section of 'Atonement', and it features perhaps the greatest crime of all: man's inhumanity to man. McEwan has spoken often about how important the war is to him as an individual, and as a writer: his father was a solder, and as a child he grew up on army camps: 'it was such a constant presence in my childhood' he has said. In all his work, and in this part, violence is portrayed with brutal clarity because 'you either do violence or you sentimentalize it'. For McEwan it would be a crime to not show the violence of war. The same is true of Part Three where some of the most moving scenes involve the consequences of the war, when innocent soldiers had to be treated for terrible injuries.

But, of course, Briony's crime is central to the book, and we cannot understand the main themes of 'Atonement' unless we recognise it as something done with intent. Briony herself is unforgiving in her evaluation of what she does, admitting as the narrator herself:

'She would never be able to console herself that she was pressured or bullied. She never was.'

And yet the irony is that we are never sure what crimes have been committed: presumably she lies under oath, except that it is left vague as to when she begins to realise that she was wrong in accusing Robbie of rape. Furthermore, the rape itself is never described as such, although it is clear that Lola has been assaulted: but was it consensual? Did intercourse take place? We never find out. For a novel with crime at its centre there is a surprising lack of unambiguous criminal acts. What McEwan seems more interested in are the wider interpretations of crime, and its consequences.

In 'Atonement' McEwan does not limit himself to just describing a simple criminal act: for him crime manifests itself in many different ways, and only one of these involves the war. One of the novel's main literary devices is to look at different events through different eyes, and open up new perspectives. McEwan looks at crime – and its consequences – in this way: asking us to think not just of the physical injuries, but also the emotional and psychological scars that result. Very often it is these which take longer to heal. And in the case of Robbie and Cecilia it could be argued that they never find peace, except in the imagination of the author.

Examiner's commentary

- ◤ This student has a very clear understanding of the task and selects key episodes from the novel to link directly to the main argument.
- ◤ Quotations are used appropriately, whether from *Atonement* or a secondary source. (AO1)
- ◤ The student comments meaningfully on AO3 by connecting the context of the theme (crime) with the author's own background.
- ◤ The student's own views are clearly in evidence.
- ◤ The student has a clear understanding of McEwan's writing technique and the structure of the text.

If the rest of her essay reached this level of performance, it is likely she would be on course to achieve a notional grade A.

Step 2: Developing and linking: go with the flow

An essay is a very specific type of formal writing that requires an appropriate discourse structure. In the main body of your writing, you need to thread your developing argument through each paragraph consistently and logically, referring back to the terms established by the question itself, rephrasing and reframing as you go. It can be challenging to sustain the flow of your essay and keep firmly on track, but here are some techniques to help you:

- Ensure your essay doesn't disintegrate into a series of disconnected building blocks by creating a neat and stable bridge between one paragraph and the next.
- Use discourse markers – linking words and phrases like 'on the other hand', 'however', 'although' and 'moreover' – to hold the individual paragraphs of your essay together and signpost the connections between different sections of your overarching argument.
- Having set out an idea in Paragraph A, you might need to then support it in Paragraph B by providing a further example; if so, signal this to the reader with a phrase such as '**Moreover** the motif of the triangle can also be seen when …'.
- To change direction and challenge an idea begun in Paragraph A by acknowledging that it is open to interpretation, you could begin Paragraph B with something like '**On the other hand**, this view of the novel could be challenged by a feminist critic …'.
- Another typical paragraph-to-paragraph link is when you want to show that the original idea does not give the full picture. Here you could modify your original point with something like '**Although** it is possible to see Briony's revision of Part One as something which at first is confusing and also perhaps compromises the integrity of the text, such a view does not take into account the postmodernist structure of the whole text.'

Student B

This student is addressing the same question as Student A.

Crime is at the heart of 'Atonement': it features not only as a main theme but, arguably, informs the whole structure of the text. And although it is true that war crimes feature strongly in the novel, and especially in Parts 2 and 3, we have to look at the whole novel to see how widely interpreted criminal behaviour is by McEwan: the casual crimes inflicted by parents on their children (the Quinceys are described as 'refugees'), the physical assaults that Lola endures before the 'rape' at the end of Part 1, and of course Briony's crime in accusing Robbie of that assault. Such acts are criminal, if not always legally, then morally. But although these are damaging they seem to pale into insignificance when we read Part Two, which is a prolonged and visceral description of the retreat from France. It is here that the real crimes take place.

However, as we see when we finish reading the book, the pages focusing on Robbie and set in France could be 'fictitious' – inventions created by the elderly Briony after she has researched Dunkirk in the Imperial War Museum. Moreover, Part Three, which is also set during the war, but this time on the domestic front, could be said to be a more penetrating depiction of the real consequences of war, seen from the perspective of a nurse. The injuries described, and the pitiful deaths of innocent men, tell us a great deal about war.

War is a crime in this novel: as Robbie walks across France he reflects on his innocence, but also how he, as a soldier who has killed, or ignored those who have died, is as much a victim as a villain:

'Everyone was guilty, and no one was. No one would be redeemed by a change of evidence, for there weren't enough people, enough paper and pens, enough patience and peace, to take down the statements of all the witnesses and gather in the facts. The witnesses were guilty too. All day we've witnessed each other's crimes. You killed no one today? But how many did you leave to die?'

This key quotation from Part 2 shows how innocence and guilt are essential to understanding the main characters in the novel, but also how the desire for Briony to explain her crime, and to find atonement for it, shapes the whole structure of the novel. Here, war is a crime, and its consequences cannot be separated from other events in the book. The balanced antithesis of 'Everyone was guilty, and no-one was' expresses the paradoxical nature of guilt in war simply and directly and the alliterated plosives of 'there weren't enough people, enough paper and pens, enough patience and peace, to take down all the statements of all the witnesses' reinforce the sense of how widespread such crimes are. Also, the way in which the quotation culminates in questions that use the voice of an unnamed witness, as well as the second person pronoun, engage the reader directly and show how personally Robbie takes the crimes he has committed in war.

On the other hand, the fictionalised Cyril Connolly, in his rejection letter to Briony in Part Three, advises her to avoid writing about war altogether: for him 'warfare ... is the enemy of creative activity' and because 'artists are politically impotent, they must ... develop at deeper emotional levels'. It is not a view held by McEwan, and once we understand the true irony of his words, and the fact that Briony, in the final part of the book, views the author as a god of her own world, we can better understand how fully engaged a writer can be – be it politically or artistically. That said, even this god cannot erase her crime.

These criminal acts cause a succession of conflicts throughout the text, and each are interconnected: Briony's crime determines Robbie's future, but also her own. It is also interesting to note that the structure of the novel also explores conflict: each section seems to function semi-autonomously being, initially at least, only loosely linked with what has gone before and what might follow. There is, then, creative tension which operates between each section of the novel, an artistic conflict that can only be peacefully resolved by the author in the final part.

Briony's crime is not the greatest in the novel, and to see it as something functioning alone, free of endless consequences, would be a mistake. McEwan exposes how certain societies tolerate and promote crimes in order to enforce their own values: Robbie was convicted because of her testimony, but also because he was of a lower class than Marshall. Equally, the crimes we witness elsewhere in the novel are of different degrees of seriousness, but taken together they provide a dark view of human behaviour. Until, that is, the final part when Briony writes that 'the only conceivable solution would be for the past never to have happened.' This desire creates her novel.

Examiner's commentary

This student:

- expresses herself very fluently, referring to key scenes but striking a balance between what to mention, and what to develop
- creates very good cohesion between paragraphs by clearly connecting the stages of her argument
- uses well-chosen discourse markers – ' however', 'moreover', 'furthermore' – to signpost the flow of her ideas
- makes a very neat paragraph-to-paragraph link to indicate that the novel's structure is integral to understanding how important conflict is
- presents a focused and sophisticated main argument.

If the rest of her essay reached this level of performance, it is likely she would be on course to achieve a notional grade A.

Step 3: Concluding: seal the deal

As you bring your writing to a close, you need to capture and clarify your response to the given view and make a relatively swift and elegant exit. Keep your final paragraph short and sweet. Now is not the time to introduce any new points – but equally, do not just reword everything you have already said either. Neat potential closers include:

- ◥ looping the last paragraph back to something you mentioned in your introduction to suggest that you have now said all there is to say on the subject
- ◥ reflecting on your key points in order to reach a balanced overview
- ◥ ending with a punchy quotation that leaves the reader thinking
- ◥ discussing the contextual implications of the topic you have debated
- ◥ reversing expectations to end on an interesting alternative view
- ◥ stating why you think the main issue, theme or character under discussion is so central to the play
- ◥ mentioning how different audiences over time might have responded to the topic you have been debating.

Student C

This student is addressing the same question as Students A and B.

I agree with this statement a lot and we can see it in most sections of the book. The best sections of 'Atonement' are Parts Two and Three, which are both focused on the war. The other two sections of the book – set in peacetime – are very slow, and lacking in any really interesting events. Much of Part One – which is the longest section in the book – is focused on Briony and her crime, and this is the most interesting part of this section.

This crime dominates the novel: it is responsible for Robbie being sent to prison and also for him fighting (and dying) in France. So, in many ways, this crime influences the whole novel and explains why the narrator – Briony – is so determined to re-visit the scenes of her crime and try to make things better. Some of the scenes in Part Two – for example the shooting of the horses and the description of the boy's leg stuck in a tree – are really powerful, but their power resides in the fact that they are crimes: crimes against humanity, crimes against morality. We find them offensive, and this is done deliberately by McEwan. The scenes in Part Three, which is mostly set in a hospital in

London during the war, are also really powerful and tell us a lot about war.

McEwan uses a lot of literary devices to explore war — such as metaphor and also irony — and although there are moments which show how some characters are involved in conflict (for example Robbie's argument with Cecilia over the vase) they are not really developed and nothing is ever really solved. The novel turns on a number of seemingly small episodes: the breaking of the vase, the wrong letter being delivered, a false accusation made by a child, but all these and more come together to show one thing: that actions have consequences. The war is a huge manifestation of crimes, but McEwan is asking us to look more closely at each one, as well as the domestic crimes that contribute to so much human misery. However, it is because Briony seeks to avoid 'the bleakest realism' that we are provided with some hope at the end.

Examiner's commentary

This student:

- makes some good arguments about war and crime, although focuses too much on Parts 1 and 2 at the start of the essay
- fails to finish by clarifying her argument or actively debating the original task focus; the final sentence is ambiguous
- does at the end begins to consider an alternative viewpoint, but by then it is too late
- refers to literary terms such as 'metaphor' and 'irony' but does not give examples of where or how they are used, and does not directly link them to the task
- shows an increasingly sophisticated level of understanding of the question as it progresses, but the answer is uneven.

If the rest of her essay reached this level of performance, it is likely she would be on course to achieve a notional grade C.

Building skills 2: Analysing texts in detail

This section of the guide contains a range of annotated extracts from students' responses to *Atonement*. The next few pages will enable you to assess the extent to which these students have successfully demonstrated their writing skills and mastery of the Assessment Objectives, to provide you with an index by which to measure your own progress. Each extract comes with a commentary to help you identify what each student is doing well and/or what changes they would need to make to their writing to target a higher grade.

The main focus here is on how you can successfully include within your own well-structured writing clear and appropriate references to both *Atonement* itself and the ways in which other readers have responded to the novel. In an examination, of course, the 'other reading' you need to refer to consistently is the one expressed in the question itself. In a non-examined assessment unit, you will have more choice about which interpretations of the text you most want to work with — but since you have much more time and may well have written your own question title, you have even less excuse to wander off task.

Analysis in examination tasks

Student A

This student is answering a sample examination task from an AQA B paper.

'In fiction women characters are traditionally presented as victims of crime and men as villains.'

To what extent do you agree with this view? Remember to include relevant detailed exploration of McEwan's authorial methods in your answer.

The most obvious victim in 'Atonement' is Lola Quincey. It is she who is assaulted and then (we are led to believe) raped by Paul Marshall. Yet by the end of the novel Briony describes the now Lady Marshall as 'lean and fit as a racing dog', a 'Cruella de Vil' caricature of a rich wife to a 'doddery' but 'cruelly handsome plutocrat'. It could be seen that if she is a victim she has long since forgiven her abuser in return for wealth. However, as with many of the incidents that shape this novel, there are different perspectives which challenge the reader to think anew about what they have just read. If Lola is the victim, why does she not accuse her attacker? Is it really credible that she would not know the difference between Robbie

Turner and Paul Marshall? Was it in any way consensual (in Chapter 6 in Part One she and Marshall flirt with each other). Her (long-lasting) marriage to her attacker could be seen as an act of atonement by Marshall, or it could be something simpler: an act of love. We have to constantly remind ourselves that the narrator to all these incidents is not McEwan but Briony, who has her own motives for casting certain characters in a way that makes her own atonement easier. And so perhaps the real victims lie elsewhere.

One of the many strengths of 'Atonement' is that McEwan has subverted conventional power relationships to expose weaknesses in society. It is the (female) Briony who is the villain, guilty of committing a crime in full knowledge of what she was doing. While it is the (male) Robbie Turner who is her victim. It could be argued that the animosity that Briony has for Robbie springs from his rejection of her several years before the start of the novel, but this remains ambiguous. What we do know is that after Briony has read Robbie's vulgar letter to Cecilia she sees him as 'a maniac', and that something 'irreducibly … male, threatened the order of [her] household'. This suggests a premeditated desire by her to accuse Robbie of something, regardless of his innocence.

Briony acts out of revenge, and McEwan makes it very clear that she is the villain. Indeed, we can only read the novel in this way, and understand her need for atonement, if it is to make sense. Equally, though, it could be argued that Briony has also become the victim of her own actions: her family is ruined, and she spends much of her adult life as a writer seeking to redraft a tragedy that she created, but which now is too bleak for her to accept.

In the world that McEwan creates in 'Atonement' there are no moral certainties: male and female characters are equally capable of villainous acts. The key issue for the author is whether they are aware of the consequences and, if they are, if they are capable of gaining forgiveness.

Examiner's commentary

This student:

- regularly refers back to the terms of the question, and mentions McEwan as the maker of textual meaning frequently when analysing his methods and themes

- shows a secure grasp of the structure of the novel, and the intrinsic nature of authorial perspective in shaping our understanding of key events

- challenges the question's very general assumption that male and female characters conform to certain stereotypes – the challenge will be expanded on throughout the essay

- uses appropriate connectives like 'undoubtedly', 'and yet', 'however'

- forges a very clear link between two paragraphs that achieves cohesion and thus reassures the examiner that he is still fully on task

- uses the modal verb phrases such as 'it could be argued' together with the subtle verb 'suggests' to show an awareness that textual meanings are unfixed

- embeds short snippets of quotation within sentences seamlessly, so that the flow of his writing is not disrupted

- quotes frequently and relevantly – the quotations referring to Lola lead us into an exploration of both characterisation and the key theme of forgiveness.

If the rest of his examination answer reached this level of performance, it is likely the candidate would be on course to achieve a notional grade A.

Student B

This student is answering a sample examination task from an AQA A paper, Paper 1:

You must write about two texts: one prose and one poetry text (at least two poems must be covered). One of these texts must be written pre-1900.

'Compare how the authors of two texts you have studied present ideas about love.'

Ian MacEwan, William Blake and Andrew Marvell present very strong ideas of love. In 'Atonment' McEwan explores various forms of love: Briony had a crush on Robbie; Robbie loves Cecilia and she loves him; Paul Marshall loves Lola and they end up getting married. There is also the love between the Talles family, but that doesn't last once Robbie has been sent to jail. Each of these different representations of love share a common characteristic: they are all flawed.

Love is a very powerful emotion in 'Atonement'. When Robbie and Cecilia have sex in the library they begin to fall in love. But you could say that they were attracted to each other before then – going back to even when they were children. I don't think this is very believable because they are bound to have noticed these things before. When they do fall in love though they remain faithful to each other, even when Robbie is found guilty of rape. She keeps saying to him 'Come back. I will be faithful' this keeps Robbie going through France. Of all the characters who experience love in the novel it is Robbie and Cecilia who appear to have something genuine.

Briony doesn't really seem to love anyone in the novel. She acts selfishly and destroys Robbie's life. At the end she tries to make things better by altering the ending. This is postmodernist. But the reality is that Robbie was wrongly convicted and then dies alone in France. This tells us something about the time the novel was set, and it also tells us more about how fragile McEwan believes love is. Briony does marry, but she finishes her life alone, desperately trying to atone for the love she has ruined.

Marshall and Lola seem to love each other. They stay married until the very end of the book, even though he is creepy and probably raped her. This shows that she forgave him, that he found some sort of forgiveness. This provides the reader with hope at the end: like Cecilia and Robbie we see a couple who have remained committed to each other, despite what has happened. It is Briony who questions their marriage, but we know that she has her own reasons for doing so. In this novel love is complex and never something perfect.

Love is also important in Andrew Marvell's 'To His Coy Mistress'. In this poem the poet appears to be polite and courteous, but actually his intentions are clear to the reader: he wants his mistress to have sex with him. As in 'Atonement' a key theme is time: the narrator in this poem says that if they had all the time in the world then they would be able to talk at length about their love, and he would spend at least 'a hundred years' her eyes. But there isn't enough time, and so, while they are still young, they should 'tear' at their pleasures. This reminds us of the passion that Robbie and Cecilia share. In William Blake's 'Garden of Love' there is a very different form of love to the love we see in the other texts. This is the love between the priests and God, but not between human beings.

> ### Examiner's commentary
>
> Note how this student:
>
> ▾ does not fully understand the different aspects of the question
>
> ▾ fails to develop a sophisticated argument, or to put a number of different arguments, at the centre of the answer
>
> ▾ makes several basic technical errors with punctuation and grammar – including getting characters' names wrong, the author's name wrong, and also the title of the novel wrong (once)
>
> ▾ occasionally writes about characters as if they are real, rather than McEwan being the maker of textual meaning
>
> ▾ does not link paragraphs or develop arguments
>
> ▾ does make several perceptive points about aspects of the theme of love in the novel
>
> ▾ quotes only once (although not embedded, and gets this key quotation wrong) and uses no literary terms
>
> ▾ does explore AO3 at the end of the penultimate paragraph
>
> ▾ *does* make meaningful connections between McEwan's text and Marvell's poem, shows a sound understanding of how authors shape meaning and uses some limited use of primary quotations in linking the texts.
>
> **If the rest of her examination answer reached this level of performance, it is likely she would be on course to achieve a notional grade B.**

Analysis in non-exam assessments

Student C

This student is studying OCR's A Level in English Literature. This is an extract from Task 1: a close reading of four pages from her set text.

Consider the opening four pages of 'Atonement' in which McEwan introduces us to Briony Tallis, the main character in the novel. In what ways does McEwan develop her character and to what extent does it prepare us for the complex structure of the novel?

The opening four pages to Ian McEwan's 'Atonement' is a deliberately measured start to this highly complex novel. In fact, we can only fully appreciate why an author well known for his dramatic openings (such as in 'Enduring Love') has chosen to begin in this way: that fuller reading is revealed in Part Three when Cyril

Connolly critiques Briony's first draft of 'Two figures by a fountain' and compares it, unfavourably, to Virginia Woolf's writing style. Connolly complains that although 'the crystalline present moment' is a 'worthy subject in itself' it can lack 'forward movement'.

However, the opening pages to any novel are important, and McEwan must have faced a difficult choice between writing a pastiche of Woolf's style or adapting it so that it does appeal to a modern reader more accustomed to the novels of Ian Macabre (the nickname he has attracted because of his exploration of dark subjects) than Woolf and her contemporaries. There is, of course, the added complication which is that in the context of this novel the 'author' is Briony, not McEwan. The events described have been experienced – and affected – by her. In light of this, the narrative position is not fixed, and although it begins as a conventional, third person realist narrative, the focus and emphasis changes over the course of Part One, with at times the voice being closer to free indirect style that is indistinguishable from Briony's own perspective. This implies a more intimate story, and something closer to the central character than we might originally have thought.

It is this intimacy which should alert us to the changes that are to come later in the novel, both to the narrative position, and to how we evaluate Part One. The worlds that she creates, 'burrowing in the delicious gloom of her canopy bed, when she made her heart thud with luminous, yearning fantasies' appear innocuous at this early stage, but become damaging later on when she accuses Robbie of raping Lola. However, once we discover that Briony is the narrator of this passage, and not McEwan, we see each statement as something more than purely descriptive: each insight, each display of innocence, is to some extent an explanation of her behaviour, written after her crime, and once we understand this, we realise that even the most innocent of actions has been re-evaluated by the main character who, more than anything else, seeks atonement from not only Robbie and Cecilia, but also her readers. These opening pages not only 'set the scene', but they also, on reflection, establish it as a novel about the process of writing, and rewriting.

Because this is a novel about writing it is appropriate that it starts with a play. Briony's melodrama – 'The Trials of Arabella' – has just been completed in a 'tempest of composition'. It has been written to welcome back Briony's brother, Leon, to the family home, and it also allows the visiting cousins a chance to perform. Even at this early stage there are moments when we become aware that these are scenes being reflected upon ('Briony was hardly to know it then …'), and there is also a sense of self-invention as Briony imagines herself as the successful author she would later become. The past merges with the present and future in a way that only fully coheres in the novel's final pages.

We do learn a lot about Briony from these first pages: McEwan writes of her obsession to 'have the world just so', and in fact it is her 'controlling demon', an image which will later take on more sinister connotations when she commits her crime that condemns Robbie to prison. In many ways her actions at the end of this chapter are motivated by a desire to make sense of an adult world, to interpret it in one way, to have it 'just so'. McEwan shows us how disastrous this approach is, especially in someone so young.

Examiner's commentary

Note how this student:

- ▼ immediately shows a clear understanding of the whole text, and how it shapes these first pages

- ▼ makes appropriate references to other works by McEwan, and also a secure understanding of his reputation. This might not have been entirely relevant if it had been used to satisfy AO3, but this develops our understanding of the context in which McEwan is writing.

- ▼ uses phrases such as 'in many ways', 'however', 'in light of this', together with the subtle verb 'implies', to flag up the idea of multiple interpretations of text

- ▼ shapes her essay by ranging across *Atonement*, bringing in appropriate evidence to support her analysis

- ▼ develops her argument with each paragraph

- ▼ shows real confidence in discussing complex ideas about point of view and voice, and how they have been manipulated by Briony (and McEwan)

- ▼ has a sophisticated understanding of the structure of the whole text, and how we can only understand Part One in light of reading London 1999: subtle integration of complex literary technique

- ▼ focuses effectively on a key quotation about Briony and uses it to explore an important aspect of her character, before going on to consider this in relation to an important aspect of the novel's structure.

If the rest of her examination answer reached this level of performance, it is likely she would be on course to achieve a notional grade A.

Extended commentaries
Briony's crime, pp. 156–7

The opening sentence of this chapter is both blunt and, on reflection, illuminating. McEwan appears to be unambiguous in his description of Briony's actions as 'a crime', but it is only on finishing the novel that we learn that Briony is the author herself: it is she who judges her own behaviour in this highly moralistic way, and explains her need for atonement. Understanding that Briony is the narrator, rather than McEwan, explains aspects of the narrative – such as the often sympathetic tone of the writing – that we find here.

In London 1999, Briony admits that, even as an old woman, there is still the 'busy, priggish, conceited little girl' who still suffers from 'ridiculous vanity', and these characteristics can be found in this important passage. The language is deliberately melodramatic as if to partly explain her actions (she is 'conscious that she was sharing the night with a maniac') but also to emphasise her natural propensity to create a fictionalised narrative (verbs such as 'ducked', 'knifing' and 'swung', and adverbs such as 'boldly' exaggerate what is, in effect, a walk in the dark).

We have seen this predilection for melodrama before: it is no coincidence that her play, *The Trials of Arabella*, belongs in this genre. Melodrama allows Briony to imagine a number of extreme possibilities, almost at the same moment (and certainly on the same page), and they can veer between the innocent (the twins could be 'fooling with the hoses') or the sinister (or they could be 'floating face down in death'). Briony spends much of Part One moving between her childlike world of innocence and imagination to the more adult world of experience and harsh reality, desperately reaching for the latter but still too young to cope with what this might entail. This passage marks 'another entry, a moment of coming into being'.

At this stage in the narrative Briony is empowered to describe anything: she is the 'God' of the final part, filled with the 'absolute power' to decide fates. Until this moment Briony's acts of imagination have no consequences for anybody else, but that is about to change. As we read we have a growing sense that Briony has already decided Robbie's fate: she describes him as a 'maniac' three times, a man with a 'dark, unfulfilled heart', something which we as readers know not to be true.

Intrinsic to understanding the importance of this passage is McEwan's use of voice and point of view. There is a subtle, slow change from the conventional third-person narrative to something closer to free indirect style that is at times detached but also personal.

For example, during the play's rehearsals Briony sits down on the floor, exhausted by the effort of having to keep her cousins engaged in her text.

We see her described externally – her 'back to one of the tall built-in toy cupboards … her knees out straight before her'. But McEwan's gaze begins to become more intrusive, as if a camera begins to zoom in. Briony focuses on her finger, and contemplates how consciousness can make it move:

> The mystery was in the instant before it moved, the dividing moment between not moving and moving, when her intention took effect. It was like a wave breaking. If she could only find herself at the crest, she thought, she might find the secret of herself, that part of her that was really in charge.

This goes beyond a conventional, third-person narration: it is a psychological study deliberately written with a more intimate understanding of the character's mind. The passage goes on to explore the nature of consciousness itself, but is done so in a language that a child of Briony's age could not possibly have. In other words, the elderly Briony is developing, creating, embellishing an idea which a young girl could conceivably have, but lacks the experience and vocabulary to reveal its complexity to an adult readership.

Briony reveals an informed sense of foreknowledge that puts the crime she is about to commit into context: she does it, it seems, with a full knowledge of its consequences, that would be impossible to possess if the narrative only remained fixed in the 'crystalline present moment' referred to by Cyril Connolly in Part Three. She knows that she is about to be the 'object of adult hatred' and for her, tellingly, it is 'a promotion', an 'initiation into a solemn new world' that is 'horrifying' but inevitable. In other words, it is worth the damage. We watch, with a growing sense of alarm, at what is inevitably going to destroy Robbie. Knowing this, in retrospect, explains the added sense of an 'underlying pull of simple narrative' that Connolly suggests would make Part One more interesting. It also explains her desire for atonement.

This multi-layered passage is not a conventional description of a young girl searching for the twins and stumbling across Lola and her abuser; or at least, if it originally was, it has been revised by an author aware of its literary limitations, and also with a need for public forgiveness. The opening sentence is illuminating because her action could not have been judged a crime from the narrative position that Briony appears to adopt at that moment. Such nuanced shifts in tone, and perspective, allow the reader to better grasp the full complexity and importance of this pivotal moment in the novel.

Robbie's final moments, pp. 264–5

This is one of the most unusual – but effective – passages in the novel. Although *Atonement* is told, for the most part, in a conventional, third-person, past-tense narrative, these pages are among the least realist of all. The dreamlike tone allows McEwan to move across themes and symbols in a style close to stream of consciousness: sentences seem unconnected, and themes are only partially explored by transient images and undeveloped symbolism. It has its own poetic beauty but, again, the real power of these pages can only be fully appreciated when we have finished the novel and realise that these are Robbie's final moments. On an initial reading these pages are at times surreal and otherworldly. But once Briony has told us that Robbie died of septicaemia, they take on a more elegiac, sombre tone that is immensely moving.

In that final part Briony admits that she loves the 'little things, the pointillist approach to verisimilitude', and to some extent this descriptive style – in which apparently unconnected images are built up to create a coherent picture – is in evidence here. The figurative and literal cross over: the passage begins with Robbie 'falling now', but that could refer to sleep or death. Nettle's 'soothing whisper' is something closer to the tone a mother would adopt with a sleepy child, rather than the words we know have just been exchanged ('Too much noise, Guv'nor'). And if there is a theme in this passage it is that of rescue, both physical and emotional.

Point of view shot: a shot taken from the perspective of a character in the film; it allows the audience to see through the character's eyes.

The past, the present and the future dissolve into each other with a quality that is cinematic in its construction: fade outs and **POVs** (point of view shots) combine to track different episodes and ideas, but each contribute to a coherent depiction of slow death, and a failure to be rescued. As the world disintegrates around him Robbie clings to the hope that 'order would prevail': the sense of purpose that the army has instilled in him, which has forced him to keep marching, merges again (earlier Robbie has 'tramped', counting out each step as 'five iambs and an anapaest') with the 'free, unruly spirits' of the poets he has studied in Cambridge, poets such as Auden, Yeats and Housman, each of whom have been alluded to on his escape from the German forces. Words shape his final moments: clichés, so often deployed when original thought becomes too difficult, crowd in on moments of revelation ('no breaking ranks, no rushing the boats, no first come first served ... it was the tranquil sea, and now he himself was calm').

There is one phrase that reoccurs: 'I'll wait for you, come back'. These words are described as 'elemental', the 'reason he had survived'. They are sensuous, connecting him with the sights ('he could not forget that green dress'), sounds ('he ... turned at the sound of her steps') and touches ('the feel of the gravel ... he could feel it now') of their original context – the moment of his arrest for rape, the final words Cecilia said to him before he is driven away by the police. The description of their exchange is the most realist passage in these pages: they describe in intimate detail the exchange between these two central characters, reiterating that the moment in the library – their 'secret' – was theirs forever. Time, another important theme in this passage, begins to close in on Robbie, but this moment has survived everything, and 'time would show she really meant it'.

His final words are, ironically, a promise to speak no more: on the surface, before we reread these pages in the light of Briony's revelation that he dies at this point, they are a simple promise to Nettle to stop disturbing the sleeping men around him. But they take on a new poignancy when we realise their true importance. Robbie dies with Cecilia's words in his mind: he never does return to England, but in some respects he never left her, nor she him. This is the ending that Briony wants, and one which avoids 'the bleakest realism' that is the truth. The lovers are finally reunited, if not in life, then at least in each other's thoughts. Her words, her promise to 'refuse all other men' has 'rescued' Robbie.

In all works of literature, meaning is influenced by the form of the text. The style adopted in this passage reflects Robbie's state of mind. As his grasp of reality begins to fragment so does this passage's structure: sentences break up, and sometimes only stand as semi-autonomous images ('Whiter than the mist'). In McEwan's clever manipulation of structure and perspective, *Atonement* is postmodernist in style: it reveals the processes of its different parts in order for us to re-evaluate the act of creation itself. Nowhere is this more the case than in these very moving pages.

Top ten quotations

Before studying this section, you should identify your own 'top ten' quotations – i.e. those phrases or sentences that seem to capture a key theme or aspect of the text most aptly and memorably – and clearly identify what it is about your choices that makes each one so significant. No two readers of *Atonement* will select exactly the same set, and it will be well worth discussing (and perhaps even having to defend) your choices with the other students in your class.

When you have done this, look carefully at the following list of top ten quotations and consider each one's possible significance within the novel. How might each be used in an essay response to support your exploration of various elements or readings of *Atonement*? Consider what these quotations tell us about Ian McEwan's ideas, themes and methods as well as how far they may contribute to various potential ways of interpreting the text.

1 'At this stage in her life Briony inhabited an ill-defined transitional space between the nursery and adult worlds which she crossed and recrossed unpredictably.' (p. 141)

> ▼ One of the key themes in the novel is the conflict between innocence and experience, and two characters personify this: Lola Quincey and Briony Tallis. Although Lola behaves in a more overtly adult-like manner, Briony is also moving from being a child to an adolescent. Unlike Lola, who expresses these changes in an overtly sexual way, Briony uses her imagination to manipulate others. But just as Lola is not aware of the consequences of her actions, Briony, too, is not mature enough to understand how her interpretation of events is not the only one possible. At this point in the novel only Robbie can read her accurately; tragically, and ironically, it is also he who most suffers from her own misreading of events.

2 'Within the half hour Briony would commit her crime.' (p. 156)

> ▼ We are left in no doubt from this statement that Briony's actions are criminal. She acts with a full knowledge of what she is doing. Of course what she does is, in legal terms, a crime: she has, under oath in a court of law, falsely accused someone of a crime they did not commit. But in a novel in which God and religion barely feature, it also reminds us that a sense of morality, founded in Judeo-Christian countries on the Ten Commandments, has been broken. The Ninth Commandment is 'Thou shall not bear false witness against thy neighbour', and this is precisely what Briony does. Crucially, it is Briony herself, as the author, who describes her action as a crime, and because she judges it in this way we can better understand why she seeks atonement.

'She would never be able to console herself that she was pressured or bullied. She never was.' (p. 170)

▼ Briony is not an innocent child who acts with good intentions: instead, as McEwan goes on to explain, she acts in full knowledge of what she is doing. Briony 'marched herself into the labyrinth of her construction' and was 'too keen to please' to insist on making her own way back. Her inability to find consolation, to blame others, explains why, as the 'author', she has to rewrite events to make them more hopeful, and also to seek forgiveness: only as an adult can she begin to find a route back to something which might atone for her actions. In addition, although this tells us a great deal about Briony's actions it also suggests at an early stage that what might appear to be a conventional third-person narrative written in the past tense is something more complex: it looks ahead, shows foresight, and changes our perspective of both events and this character.

3

'I'll wait for you. Come back.' (p. 213)

▼ Robbie's hatred of Briony is balanced by his love for her sister. This phrase, first uttered by Cecilia just before he is taken away by the police and charged for the rape of Lola, begins to take on a greater power than they originally contained. For Robbie they are repeated regularly, like a mantra, recalled to sustain him in prison, as he marches through France and in his dying moments. It is closely intertwined with hope, of 'getting back', not just to England but also to his previous life. Cecilia writes these words in her first letter to him from Liverpool ('quoting herself. She knew he would remember'), and it is how she ends every letter she writes to him. These are her last words to him in her final letter. As he dies he recalls these words and when she first says them, 'and the memory of when she had said it … he had come to treat like a sacred site'. The words have become a sacrament to him, containing their own innate truth and beauty. They are the last words he recalls before he dies, and in a novel where there are so many lies, their power reside in something simple: 'she meant it'.

4

'To be cleared would be a pure state. He dreamed of it like a lover, with a simple longing.' (p. 228)

▼ Atonement is a public act, for both the accuser and the accused. Robbie Turner dreams of having his name cleared so that, in many respects, he can begin again. As he moves through France, seeing death and destruction around him, he seeks a return to a state of innocence that he lost when he was arrested for rape. It is, for him,

5

'elemental', a fundamental process that will effectively rewrite the past, forcing everyone 'to adjust their thinking'. It is an idealised state, inseparable from his vision of Cecilia. However, as we shall see, only Briony the author can rewrite the past to change our views, and for Robbie such a deliverance comes too late.

6

'Yes, she was just a child. But not every child sends a man to prison with a lie. Not every child is so purposeful and malign, so consistent over time, never wavering, never doubted.' (pp. 228–9)

> In a novel that deliberately blurs the lines between the characters' thoughts and those of the narrator, this passage is telling. It is written in free indirect style and is as close to Robbie's voice as we can get without the narrative moving into the first person. However, once we have finished reading the novel we know that it is Briony who writes this, and so it becomes semi-autobiographical. Just as she condemns herself for the 'crime' she commits, so she develops this idea of confession, which is so integral to atonement. Robbie's hatred of Briony is anticipated by her on p. 156, where she describes it as a necessary 'initiation into a solemn new world'. Although this 'horrified' her she still perseveres with her actions. Here we see the consequences, but we also understand the extent of Briony's self-awareness as well. The unambiguous words and phrases in this quotation – 'lie', 'purposeful', 'malign', 'never wavering', 'never doubted' – underline the seriousness of her actions.

7

'It was still an innocent time … The dead were not yet present, the absent were presumed alive. The scene was dreamlike in its normality.' (p. 287)

> Robbie's physical journey across France in Part Two runs parallel with Briony's personal journey from adolescence to adult. These two worlds offer two different perspectives of the war: Part Two is ostensibly male and set overseas, but Part Three describes the more domestic, female setting of a hospital effectively run by women. There are other differences, which further explore important themes in the novel, and they are suggested in this quotation. Innocence and experience often conflict, and the time described by McEwan is deliberately more complex than a cursory reading might suggest: if this is an innocent time for London it is about to be shattered by the influx of casualties from the war. But in a novel that constantly challenges us to re-evaluate what is true and false, who is alive and who is dead, this captures that sense of narrative ambiguity. It is arguable that the dead can ever be 'present', even when they are physically with us, and in what is clearly a subtle reference to Robbie, the absent might be presumed to be alive – but such hopes can often

be misguided. As we have seen from the final pages of the last part, what is normal and what is not, what is a dream and what is waking certainty, what is a lie and what is the truth, remain unfixed during wartime, and unstable in this novel.

'The crystalline present moment is of course a worthy subject in itself … However, such writing can become precious when there is no sense of forward movement.' (p. 312)

8

▼ Cyril Connolly's rejection letter to Briony in Part Three of *Atonement* is a pivotal point in the novel. McEwan has hinted elsewhere in the text that the structure of this novel is not as conventional as it might first appear; furthermore, the subtle shifts in perspective suggests a different narrator from McEwan himself. This letter profoundly alters our reading of the novel. It also forces us to reread and reconsider Part One. Connolly's criticism reveals to us why Part One has such a very different style to the rest of the book: it is highly detailed, with long passages analysing apparently unimportant events (such as when Briony contemplates how her hand, the 'fleshy spider on the end of her arm' obeys her). Even with her revisions Part One remains influenced by Virginia Woolf, and this explains its pacing, and it deliberate lack of forward momentum. Connolly's words bring it into focus for the reader, and also explains the sudden shift in style in Part Two.

'Now she had seen him walk across the room, the other possibility, that he could have been killed, seemed outlandish, against all the odds. It would have made no sense … What deliverance.' (p. 338)

9

▼ In the final part of *Atonement* Briony admits that what *really* happened was too dark to 'constitute an ending'. By imagining a different ending, and one that brings Robbie fully to life, she allows herself and her readers to escape 'the service of the bleakest realism'. Within a universe defined by the laws the author alone can create, such changes do make sense, and in such a world, where the author is God, only the author can provide such deliverance. There is a logic to this, and it makes sense, but it also undermines all other laws that the reader expects, and observes in fiction as much as in life. This breaks those bonds. This challenge to such conventions is a deliberate act of subversion by McEwan, and how we respond to it can determine both our understanding of the novel, its purpose and structure.

10 'The problem these fifty-nine years has been this: how can a novelist achieve atonement when, with her absolute power of deciding outcomes, she is also God? There is no one, no entity or higher form that she can appeal to, to be reconciled with, or that can forgive her. There is nothing outside her.' (p. 371)

> *Atonement* is a novel as much concerned with the process of writing as the events the writing describes. For Briony – and McEwan – the question of who stands above the writer to judge him or her remains unanswered and, possibly, unanswerable. The fates of all of Briony's characters reside in her hands, but what sense of duty does this responsibility carry with it to readers? Should the integrity of the narrative be preserved? Or should the author seek to rewrite each draft until 'atonement' is finally achieved? Should uncomfortable 'truths' – such as the inconvenient deaths of Robbie and Cecilia – be erased to provide a happier ending? Verisimilitude is not essential to Briony: as she says on p. 360, 'if I really cared so much about facts, I should have written a different kind of book'. She is a self-confessed 'unreliable narrator', and what we have just read, and assumed to be 'true', only exists subjectively. As this quotation suggests, if forgiveness is ultimately beyond the author perhaps the most she can hope for is aspiring to do so. Perhaps 'the attempt was all'.

Taking it further

At the time of going to press these articles were accessible online. If their locations have moved try searching for keywords. For example, 'Kermode + Point of View + London Review'

Page references in this guide refer to the 2002 Vintage edition of *Atonement*.

Reviews and literary criticism

- Phil Baker A note of apology; review of Atonement, The Daily Telegraph, 15 September 2001,
  www.telegraph.co.uk/culture/4725616/A-note-of-apology.html

- Geoff Dyer 'Who's Afraid of Influence'; review of Atonement, The Guardian, 22 September 2001,
  www.theguardian.com/books/2001/sep/22/fiction.ianmcewan

- Brian Finney 'Briony's stand against oblivion: Ian McEwan's Atonement',
  http://web.csulb.edu/~bhfinney/mcewan.html

- Mel Gussow 'Atoning for his past'; The Age, 5 May 2002,
  www.theage.com.au/articles/2002/05/03/1019441435182.html

- Frank Kermode 'Point of View'; London Review of Books, September 2001,
  www.lrb.co.uk/v23/n19/frank-kermode/point-of-view

- Hermione Lee 'If your memories serve you well…'; The Observer, 23 September 2001,
  www.theguardian.com/books/2001/sep/23/fiction.bookerprize2001

- Charles McGrath 'On Writers and Writing'; The New York Times, 27 October 2002,
  www.nytimes.com/2002/10/27/books/on-writers-and-writing-not-quite-right-for-our-pages.html

- Daniel Mendelsohn 'Unforgiven'; New York Magazine, March 2002,
  http://nymag.com/nymetro/arts/books/reviews/5776

- Claire Messud 'The Beauty of the Conjuring'; Atlantic Monthly, March 2002,
  www.theatlantic.com/past/docs/issues/2002/03/messud.htm

- Laura Miller 'Atonement by Ian McEwan'; Salon, 21 March 2002,
  www.salon.com/2002/03/21/mcewan_3

- John Mullen Book Club: a three-part series on *Atonement* published in *The Guardian*:

  'Part One: domestic space'; 8 March 2013,
  www.theguardian.com/books/2003/mar/08/ianmcewan

'Part Two: prolepsis'; 15 March 2013,
www.theguardian.com/books/2003/mar/15/ianmcewan

'Part Three: the weather'; 22 March 2013,
www.theguardian.com/books/2003/mar/22/ianmcewan

- John Updike 'Flesh on Flesh'; The New Yorker; 4 March 2002,
www.newyorker.com/magazine/2002/03/04/flesh-on-flesh

- David Wiegand 'Stumbling into fate'; San Francisco Chronicle,
10 March 2002,
www.sfgate.com/books/article/Stumbling-into-fate-Accidents-and-choices-trip-2866997.php

Interviews

- Adam Begley 'The Art of Fiction No.173'; The Paris Review, Summer 2002,
www.theparisreview.org/interviews/393/the-art-of-fiction-no-173-ian-mcewan

- Kate Kellaway 'At home with his worries'; The Observer, September 2001,
www.theguardian.com/books/2001/sep/16/fiction.ianmcewan

- Zadie Smith 'Zadie Smith talks with Ian McEwan'; The Believer, August 2005,
www.believermag.com/issues/200508/?read=interview_mcewan

- Matthew Stadlen 'Five Minutes With: Ian McEwan'; BBC, 9 November 2013,
www.youtube.com/watch?v=ewMPFzCUQF0

- Daniel Zalewski 'The Background Hum'; The New Yorker, 23 February 2009,
www.newyorker.com/magazine/2009/02/23/the-background-hum

Books

- Ian McEwan, *Atonement*, Vintage Books, 2002
- Margaret Reynolds and Jonathan Noakes, *Ian McEwan: The Essential Guide*, Vintage, 2002

Articles and other resources

- An article and interview with the British Humanist Association:
https://humanism.org.uk/about/our-people/patrons/ian-mcewan

- An article by Ian McEwan: 'The Law vs. Religious Belief', The Guardian,
5 September 2015,
www.theguardian.com/books/2014/sep/05/ian-mcewan-law-versus-religious-belief

- Wikipedia http://en.wikipedia.org/wiki/Atonement_(novel)

Film and related websites

2007: *Atonement* directed by Joe Wright, screenplay by Christopher Hampton. Starring James McAvoy, Harriet Walter, Keira Knightley, Benedict Cumberbatch, Saoirse Ronan

❧ IMDB www.imdb.com/title/tt0783233/?ref_=ttfc_fc_tt

❧ Official movie website www.focusfeatures.com/atonement/articles

STUDY AND REVISE
for AS/A-level

Read, **analyse** and **revise** your set texts throughout the course to achieve your very best grade, with support at every stage from expert teachers and examiners.

Your year-round course companions for English literature

Each book contains:
- In-depth analysis of the text, from characterisation and themes to form, structure and language
- Thought-provoking tasks that develop your critical skills and personal response to the text
- Critical viewpoints to extend your understanding and prepare you for higher-level study

Titles in the series:
- A Room with a View
- A Streetcar Named Desire
- AQA A Poetry Anthology
- Atonement
- King Lear
- Measure for Measure
- Othello
- Seamus Heaney: Selected Poems
- Skirrid Hill
- Tess of the D'Urbervilles
- The Duchess of Malfi
- The Great Gatsby
- The Handmaid's Tale
- The Taming of the Shrew
- The Tempest
- The Wife of Bath's Tale
- The Winter's Tale
- Top Girls
- Wuthering Heights

£8.99 each

View the full series and order online at www.hoddereducation.co.uk/studyandrevise